THE
SMALL GARDEN
BOOK

THE
SMALL GARDEN
BOOK

Peter McHoy

A practical guide to
successful gardening in small spaces

BARNES
&NOBLE
BOOKS
NEW YORK

Above: The change in levels and types of flooring add several different dimensions to this small garden.

This edition published by Barnes & Noble, Inc., by arrangement with Anness Publishing Limited

1998 Barnes & Noble Books

M 10 9 8 7 6 5 4 3 2 1

ISBN 0-7607-1100-3

Produced by Anness Publishing Limited
Hermes House
88–89 Blackfriars Road
London SE1 8HA

Publisher: Joanna Lorenz
Project Editor: Clare Nicholson
Commissioned Photography: John Freeman
Design: Patrick McLeavey and Partners

Printed and bound in Singapore by Star Standard Industries Pte. Ltd.

Page one: Containers can be used to give year-round color in a small garden.

Page two: The frame of this arch has been beautifully disguised with climbing roses.

Page three: A beautiful container adds a splash of color to a tiny garden.

CONTENTS

ABOVE: *This charming statue and pond create a peaceful mood.*

INTRODUCTION

SMALL GARDENS CAN STILL HAVE A BIG IMPACT, and this book shows you how to get the best from a limited area. Size is comparative of course, and if your gardening is confined to a tiny backyard or a balcony, even a small town garden can seem large. On the other hand, a medium-sized country garden may appear small to the owner of a large estate. But whether you garden on a rooftop, or you have a fairly typical small town garden or a larger plot that simply seems small to you, this book offers ideas and solutions.

Making the most of a small space depends partly on design and partly on planting. If you want a low-maintenance garden the emphasis should be on hard landscaping and the use of ground cover and low-maintenance plants. If you are a plant collector, a design with the emphasis on planting space will be important . . . but choosing the right plants in proportion to the available space is vital.

You will find lots of ideas for redesigning a small garden, from initial ideas to execution. But sometimes only minor modifications to your existing garden are necessary for a transformation, and the section on features and structures has plenty of thought-provoking ideas that you might like to consider.

Choosing appropriate plants can be the key to ensuring a small garden design works well. In the third section of the book you will find hundreds of recommended plants, arranged by use or purpose – from plants for color theme beds and borders, and those providing color in the cold months, to those grown for shade (a particular problem in small gardens) or fragrance. Many plants have more than a single role, of course, so to avoid repetition and to make space for more plants, multiple entries have been thoroughly cross-referenced.

Size is especially important in a small garden, so we have given an indication of likely heights and spreads. In the case of herbaceous plants these are typical dimensions after a couple of years, but for slower-growing trees and shrubs they are the probable size after 10–15 years. Bear in mind, however, that dimensions can be no more than a crude guide. Heights can vary greatly, according to soil, position, and local climate. Some trees and shrubs can be kept compact by regular pruning – for example, buddleias and eucalyptus are both too tall for a small garden if left unpruned, but will make compact shrubs with a good shape if cut back severely each spring.

Although you will find plenty of suggestions in the following pages, attractive gardens are not designed to a rigid formula, and there is always room for individual interpretation – and even eccentricity. Some gardens are designed to shock, some are traditional in concept, a few are strictly formal, and many are a compromise between formality and informality. There are as many garden styles as there are tastes, and the only criterion for success is whether the result pleases you personally.

Design does not become easier with decreasing size: rather, it becomes more difficult and demanding. A large garden tends to look good anyway, with the odd weedy bed going almost unnoticed among the overall impression of large lawns, stately trees and shrubs. In a small garden long vistas are out of the question and the use of trees and large shrubs is often severely limited. Every part of the garden comes under the spotlight, and errors of judgement are often emphasized.

All these handicaps can be overcome, however, and, as the illustrations in this book show, you can still make a big impact with a small garden.

OPPOSITE: *Pots and containers are a good means of incorporating herbs in a very confined space.*

ELEMENTS *of* DESIGN

Attractive small gardens seldom just happen, they are designed.
And despite the apparent contradiction, the smaller the garden,
the more important good design becomes. A small garden can be taken in
almost at a glance, and the difference between good and bad design,
attention to detail or neglect, is immediately obvious. In a small garden
there is always the temptation to try to cram in many more features
than there is really space for. Keep the design simple, stick to a style,
and follow the suggestions in this section for making a plan to scale.
Then check the effect by marking out the shapes in the garden
before you start work. This way you will be assured of success.

ABOVE: *Sometimes accommodating essentials,*
such as this tool shed, in an attractive way can
become a problem. Careful screening can help
minimize their impact.

OPPOSITE: *A small garden should not lack*
impact. Provided it is well planted and has
some strong focal points, it becomes easy to
ignore the limitations of size.

PLANNING YOUR GARDEN

Some successful gardens are worked out on the ground, in the mind's eye, perhaps visualized during a walk around the garden, or conceived in stages as construction takes place. This approach is for the gifted or very experienced, and it is far better to make your mistakes on paper first.

A major redesign can be time-consuming and expensive, especially if it involves hard landscaping (paving, walls, steps, etc.). However, simply moving a few plants is rarely enough to transform an uninspiring garden into something special. It is worth having a goal, a plan to work to, even if you have to compromise along the way. Bear in mind that you may be able to stagger the work and cost over several seasons,

but having a well thought out design ensures the garden evolves in a structured way.

Use the checklist opposite to clarify your 'needs', then decide in your own mind the *style* of garden you want. Make a note of mundane and practical considerations, like where to manage recycling and garbage, plus objects that need to be screened, such as a compost area or an unpleasant view.

Unattractive views, and necessary but unsightly objects within the garden, such as toolsheds, are a particular problem because they can dominate a small garden. Well-positioned shrubs and small trees can act as a screen. To improve the outlook instantly use a large plant in a tub.

ABOVE: *In this garden the bird feeder helps to draw the eye away from the practical corner of the garden.*

LEFT: *Make a small garden look larger than it really is by ensuring the sides are well planted and creating a striking focal point.*

OPPOSITE: *Shape and form can be as important as color in creating a stylish garden.*

LABOR-SAVING TIPS

• To minimize cost and labor, retain as many paths and areas of paving as possible, but only if they don't compromise the design.

• If you want to enlarge an area of paving, or improve its appearance, it may be possible to pave over the top and thus avoid the arduous task of removing the original.

• Modifying the shape of your lawn is easier than digging it up and relaying a new one. It is simple to trim it to a smaller shape if you want a lawn of the same area, and if you wish to change the angle or shape, it may be possible to leave most of it intact, and simply lift and relay some of the turf.

LEFT: *Strong lines and several changes of level give this small garden plenty of interest. In this kind of design, the hard landscaping is more important than the soft landscaping (the plants).*

CHOICES CHECKLIST

Before you draw up your design, make a list of requirements for your ideal garden. You will almost certainly have to abandon or defer some of them, but at least you will realize which features are most important to you.

Use this checklist at the rough plan stage, when decisions have to be made . . . and it is easy to change your mind!

Features

Barbecue	☐
Beds	☐
Borders, for herbaceous	☐
Borders, for shrubs	☐
Borders, mixed	☐
Birdbath	☐
Changes of level	☐
Fruit garden	☐
Gravelled area	☐
Greenhouse/conservatory	☐
Herb garden	☐
Lawn (mainly for decoration)	☐
Lawn (mainly for recreation)	☐
Ornaments	☐
Patio/terrace	☐
Pergola	☐
Pond	☐
Raised beds	☐
Summerhouse	☐
Sundial	☐
Vegetable plot	☐
Plus	☐

Functional features

Compost area	☐
Garage	☐
Toolshed	☐
Plus	☐

Necessities

Children's play area	☐
Climbing frame	☐
Sandpit	☐
Swing	☐
Clothes dryer	☐
Garbage or Trash Cans	☐
Plus	☐

CHOOSING A STYLE

Before sitting down with pencil and paper to sketch out your garden, spend a little time thinking about the style that you want to achieve. In many gardens plants and features are used for no other reason than that they appeal; an excellent reason, perhaps, but not the way to create an overall design that will make your garden stand out from others on the street.

The styles shown in the following six pages are not exhaustive, and probably none will be exactly right for your own garden, but they will help you to clarify your thoughts. You should know roughly what you want from your garden before you start to design it.

FORMAL APPROACH

Formal gardens appeal to those who delight in crisp, neat edges, straight lines and a sense of order. Many traditional suburban gardens are formal in outline, with rectangular lawns flanked by straight flower borders, and perhaps rectangular or circular flower beds cut into them. Such rigid designs are often dictated by the drive for the car and straight paths laid by the house builder.

Although the gardens shown here are all very different, what they have in common is a structure as important as the plants contained within it. The designs are largely symmetrical, with no pretense at creating a natural-looking environment for the plants.

The very size and shape of most small gardens limits the opportunities for natural-looking landscapes, so a formal style is a popular choice.

Parterres and knot gardens

Parterres and knot gardens often appeal to those with a sense of garden history, though in a small garden the effect can only ever be a shadow of the grand designs used by sixteenth-century French and Italian gardeners.

Parterres are areas consisting of a series of shaped beds, or compart-

ABOVE: *A knot garden. This kind of garden is not colorful, but the strong lines and formal shape, backed by a variety of greens, make it a restful place to relax.*

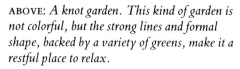

LEFT: *This small, enclosed courtyard garden balances a central focal pont with a boundary that features this dramatic entrance.*

ments, that fit together to form a pattern, often quite complex, on the ground. They were designed, often, to be viewed from the upper windows of grand houses.

Knot gardens, originally designed to be viewed from above, are similar but low-growing clipped hedges are used to form the geometric and often interwoven designs. The space between hedges can be filled with flowers or, more historically correct, colored sands or gravel, or even crushed coal if black appeals.

These are expensive gardens to create, slow to establish, and labor-intensive to maintain, but the results can be stunning. This kind of garden is unsuitable for a young family.

Formal herb gardens

Herb gardens are popular features and are much easier to create than knot gardens. Illustrations of both old and new herb gardens in books will often give you ideas for designs.

Rose gardens

A formal rose garden is easy to create, and it will look good even in its first season. To provide interest throughout the year, edge the beds with seasonal flowers and underplant the roses with spring bulbs or low-growing summer flowers.

Paved gardens

A small garden lends itself to being paved throughout. By growing most plants in raised beds or in containers, less bending is involved and many of the smaller plants are more easily appreciated. Climbers can be used to make the most of vertical space, and if you plant in open areas left in the paving, the garden can still look green.

Courtyard gardens

Space can be at a real premium in the heart of a town, but you can turn your backyard into an oasis-like courtyard garden, with floor tiles and white walls that reflect the light. Add some lush green foliage, an 'architectural' tree or large shrub, and the sound of running water. Although the plants may be few, the impact is strong.

Traditional designs

A small formal garden, with a rectangular lawn, straight herbaceous border, and rose and flower beds is still a popular choice with gardeners looking for the opportunity to grow a wide variety of plants such as summer bedding, herbaceous plants, and popular favorites such as roses. The design element is less important than the plants.

LEFT: *The use of white masonry paint can help to lighten a dark basement garden or one enclosed by high walls.*

BELOW: *This long, narrow plot has been broken up by strong lines: a useful design technique.*

INFORMAL EFFECTS

The informality of the cottage garden and the 'wilderness' atmosphere of a wild garden are difficult to achieve in a small space, especially in a town. However, with fences well clothed with plants so that modern buildings do not intrude, an informal garden can work even here.

Cottage gardens

The cottage garden style is created partly by design and the use of suitable paving materials (bricks for paths instead of modern paving slabs), and also by the choice of plants.

Relatively little hard landscaping is necessary for a cottage garden – brick paths and perhaps stepping-stones through the beds may be enough. It is the juxtaposition of 'old-fashioned' plants and vegetables that creates the casual but colorful look associated with this type of garden.

Mix annuals with perennials – especially those that will self-seed such as calendulas and *Limnanthes douglasii*, which will grow everywhere and create a colorful chaos. If flowers self-sow at the edge of the path, or between other plants, leave most of them to grow where they have chosen to put down roots.

Plant some vegetables among the flowers, and perhaps grow decorative runner beans up stakes at the back of the border.

Wildlife gardens

A small wildlife garden seems almost a contradiction in terms, but even a tiny plot can offer a refuge for all kinds of creatures if you design and plant with wildlife in mind.

Wildlife enthusiasts sometimes let their gardens 'go wild'. However, this is not necessary. A garden like this one looks well kept and pretty, yet it provides long vegetation where animals and insects can hide and find

RIGHT: *The house itself will inevitably dominate a small garden, especially when you look back towards it. Covering the walls with climbers will help it to blend in unobtrusively.*

food. There is water to attract aquatic life, and flowers and shrubs to bring the butterflies and seeds for the birds.

An orchard can also be a magnet for wildlife of many kinds.

Woodland gardens

A woodland effect is clearly impractical for a very tiny garden, but if you have a long, narrow back garden, trees and shrubs can be used very effectively. Choose quick-growing deciduous trees with a light canopy (birch trees, *Betula* species, are a good choice where there's space,

RIGHT: *The woodland effect can be delightfully refreshing on a warm spring or summer day, but works best with trees that have a tall canopy that allows plenty of light to filter through. Although a pond is attractive in this situation, care will have to be taken to remove leaves in the autumn.*

BELOW: *A pretty pond is a super way to attract wildlife, and looks especially good if well integrated into the garden like this one.*

but they can grow tall). Avoid evergreens, otherwise you will lose the benefit of the spring flowers and ferns that are so much a feature of the traditional woodland garden.

Use small-growing rhododendrons and azaleas to provide color beneath the tree canopy, and fill in with ground cover plants, naturalized bulbs such as wood anemones and bluebells, and plant woodland plants such as ferns and primroses.

Use the woodland effect to block out an unattractive view or overlooking houses. As an added bonus it is low-maintenance too.

Rocks and streams

Rock or water features alone seldom work as a 'design'. They are usually most effective planned as part of a larger scheme. Combined, however, rocks and water can be used as the central theme of a design that attempts to create a natural style in an informal garden.

Meandering meadows

Instead of the rectangular lawn usually associated with small gardens, try broadening the borders with gentle sweeps, meandering to merge with an unobstructed boundary if there is an attractive view beyond. If the distant view is unappealing, take the border around so that the lawn curves to extend beyond the point of view. Use shrubs and lower-growing border plants to create the kind of border that you might find at the edge of a strip of woodland.

Bright beds and borders

If plants are more important than the elements of design, use plenty of sweeping beds and borders, and concentrate heavily on shrubs and herbaceous plants to give the garden shape. Allow plants to tumble over edges and let them grow informally among paving.

If you want to create a strong sense of design within such a plant-oriented small garden, use focal points such as ornaments, garden seats or birdbaths.

DISTANT INFLUENCES

Professional garden designers are frequently influenced by classic styles from other countries, especially Japan, but amateurs are often nervous of trying such designs themselves. Provided you start with the clear premise that what pleases you is the only real criterion of whether something works, creating a particular 'foreign' style can be great fun. Adapt the chosen style to suit climate, landscape and the availability of suitable plants and materials.

Japanese gardens

'Real' Japanese gardens are for the purist who is prepared to give the subject much study. Raked sand and grouped stones have special meaning for those briefed in the Japanese traditions, but can be enigmatic to untrained Western eyes.

Many elements from the Japanese style can be adapted for Western tastes, however, and many gardeners are happy to introduce the essential visual elements without concern for deeper meanings. This style is easily adapted to a small space, and the uncluttered appearance makes a confined area appear larger.

Stone and gravel gardens

Although stones and rocks are widely used in Japanese gardens, they can also be key components in creating a garden which is more reminiscent of a dry river bed in an arid region – the sort of garden that you might find in a rocky, semi-desert area.

This kind of garden needs minimal maintenance, and if you choose drought-tolerant plants it should look good even in a very dry summer.

Stone gardens appeal to those with a strong sense of design, and an adventurous spirit, rather than to plant-lovers. Although the plants play a vital role in the drama of the scene, opportunities for using a wide range of plants is limited.

Gravel gardens are also a practical choice where space is limited. You can add some large boulders or rocks as focal points, and plants can be used much more freely. It is easy to plant through the gravel, and a wide range of plants can be grown in groups or as isolated specimens.

LEFT: *You don't need a lot of plants to create a Japanese-style garden. Strong hard landscaping and the restrained use of plants is a hallmark of the Japanese garden style.*

OPPOSITE TOP: *The use of formal water, painted wall and patio overhead gives this garden a Mediterranean atmosphere.*

OPPOSITE: *The dry gravel slope and the use of plants like yuccas help to create the illusion of a garden in a warm, dry climate.*

Mediterranean gardens

The illusion of a Mediterranean garden is most easily achieved in a backyard or tiny walled garden. The effect is difficult to achieve if you view neighboring homes and gardens over a low fence – they are guaranteed to kill any self-deception as to location!

Paint the walls white, or a pale color, to reflect the light and create a bright, airy feeling. If possible, include alcoves in which you can place plants, or build ledges on which you can stand pots.

Pave the area with bricks, tiles or terracotta-colored pavers – but steer clear of paving slabs. Use plenty of decorative terracotta pots and tubs.

The illusion is completed by using plenty of appropriate plants, such as pelargoniums, oleanders, bougainvilleas, and daturas (brugmansias). Stand pots of large cacti and succulents outdoors too.

The success of this kind of garden owes less to its structural design than to the use of appropriate plants, ornaments and garden furniture.

Exotic effects

You can give your garden an exotic appearance by concentrating on exotic-looking plants that are hardier than their appearance might suggest. Grow

them in pots on the patio (which will enable you to move the tender kinds to a greenhouse or conservatory, or just a sheltered position, if you garden in a cold area), or in a gravel garden.

Tough, spiky plants to consider for this kind of garden are many of the hardy yuccas, and phormiums if they grow in your area without protection. Add some agaves such as *A. americana* if you live in a very mild area or can take them indoors for the winter.

Palms are associated with warm climates, but some are tough enough to withstand moderately severe winters. *Trachycarpus fortunei* is particularly reliable. Just a few well-chosen plants can create images of far-away places.

BASIC PATTERNS

Having decided on the *style* of garden that you want, and the *features* that you need to incorporate, it is time to tackle the much more difficult task of applying them to your own garden. The chances are that your garden will be the wrong size or shape, or the situation or outlook is inappropriate to the style of garden that you have admired. The way round this impasse is to keep in mind a style without attempting to recreate it closely.

If you can't visualize the whole of your back or front garden as, say, a stone or Japanese garden, it may be possible to include the feature as an element within a more general design.

STARTING POINTS

If you analyse successful garden designs, most fall into one of the three basic patterns described below, though clever planting and variations on the themes almost always result in individual designs.

Circular theme

Circular themes are very effective at disguising the predictable shape of a rectangular garden. Circular lawns, circular patios, and circular beds are all options, and you only need to overlap and interlock a few circles to create a stylish garden. Plants fill the gaps between the curved areas and the straight edges.

Using a compass, try various combinations of circles to see whether you can create an attractive pattern. Be prepared to vary the radii and to overlap the circles if necessary.

Diagonal theme

This device creates a sense of space by taking the eye along and across the garden. Start by drawing grid lines at 45 degrees to the house or main fence. Then draw in the design, using the grid as a guide.

Rectangular theme

Most people designing use a rectangular theme – even though they may not make a conscious effort to do so. The device is effective if you want to create a formal look, or wish to divide up a long, narrow garden into smaller sections.

Circular theme

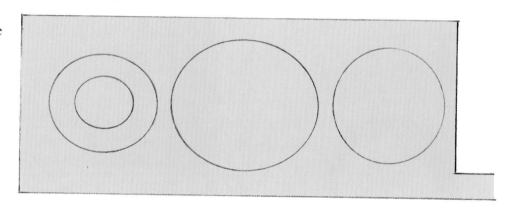

Diagonal theme

Rectangular theme

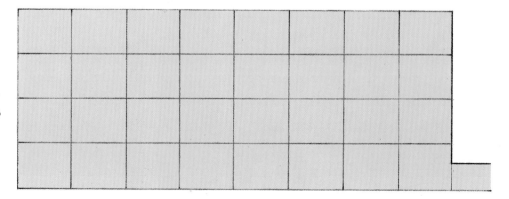

Circular theme

Diagonal theme

Rectangular theme

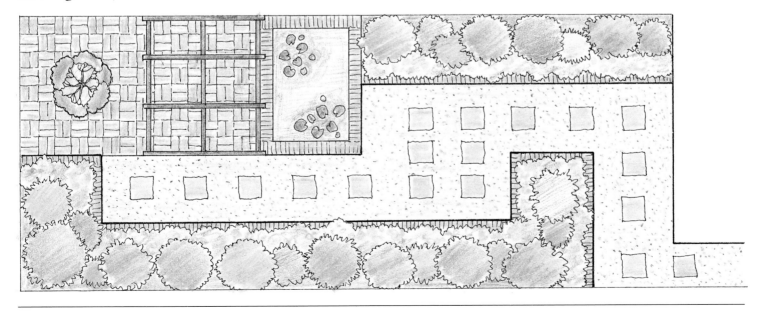

MEASURING UP

Whether designing a garden from scratch or simply modifying what you already have, you need to draw a plan of the garden as it is. A drawn plan will enable you to see the overall design clearly, and to experiment with different ideas before committing yourself to a definite option.

HOW TO MEASURE THE SITE

YOU WILL NEED:

● One, or ideally two, 100ft tape measures (unless your garden is very short). Plasticized fabric is the best material as linen stretches and steel is difficult to manipulate.
● A steel rule about 6ft long (to measure short distances).
● Pegs to mark out positions, and meat skewers to hold one end of the tape in position if working alone.
● Clip-board and pad or graph paper.
● A couple of pencils, sharpener and an eraser.

1 Make a rough visual sketch by eye. It does not have to be accurate, but try to keep existing important features roughly in proportion. Leave plenty of space on the plan for adding dimensions. If necessary, use several sheets of paper, and indicate where they join.

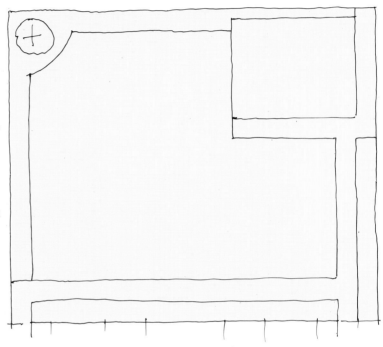

2 Choose a base line from which to start measuring. Make it a long, straight edge from which the majority of other points can be measured. A long fence or a house wall are often convenient starting points. From the straight edge or base line, measure off key points, such as the positions of windows, doors, any outbuildings, and so on. Measure out at right angles to establish the distances from the base line to the important features so that you can build the outline plan. Most key points on your plan can be established by measuring again at right angles from these right angles if necessary.

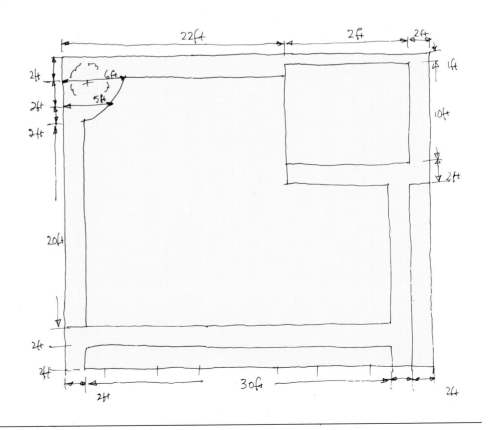

HOW TO MAKE A SCALE DRAWING

1 To make a scale drawing, choose a scale that enables you to fit the garden (or at least a self-contained section of it) onto the one sheet of graph paper. Buy large sheets of graph paper if necessary. For most small gardens, a scale of 1:50 ¼in to 1ft is about right. If your garden is large, try a scale of 1:100. Draw your base line in first, then transfer the scale measurements. When the right-angle measurements have been transferred, draw in the relevant outlines.

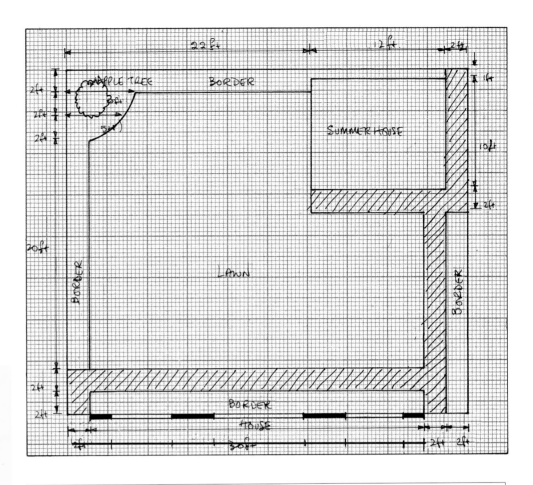

DON'T MAKE WORK

When measuring your plot, don't waste time measuring and plotting the position of features that you have no intention of retaining in your replanned garden. If you intend to remove an unsightly tree or large shrub, or to pull down a garden shed that has seen better days, leave them off your plan – they will only clutter and confuse.

SLOPES AND CONTOURS

In a large garden, slopes are often significant and may have to be taken into account. You can generally ignore gentle slopes in a small garden, or make a mental note of them.

HOW TO USE TRIANGULATION

It may not be possible to position some features or key points simply by measuring a series of right angles. These are best determined by a process known as triangulation. Using a known base, perhaps the corners of the house, simply measure the distance from two points to the position to be established. By transferring the scale distances from the two known points later, the exact position can be established. To transfer the triangulated measurements, set a compass to each of the scale distances in turn, and scribe an arc in the approximate position. Where the second arc intersects the first one, your point is established.

To fix position of tree, measure to A, then to B. Strike arcs on a scale drawing with compasses set at these measurements. Where the arcs cross shows the position of the tree in relation to the house.

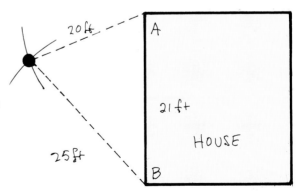

CREATING THE DESIGN

The most off-putting part of drawing up the design is the blank sheet of paper. Once this is overcome, producing alternative plans becomes fun, and there is the satisfaction of marking out the space to see the final effect in the garden. Just follow the stages below.

Stage 1: the basic grid

With the measurements transferred to graph paper you should already have a plan of your garden, showing any permanent structures and features that you want to retain.

Now superimpose onto this grid the type of design you have in mind – one based on circles, rectangles or diagonals, for example. If you are sure of the type of layout you want, draw these directly onto your plan in a second color. If you think you might change your mind, draw the grid on a transparent overlay. For most small gardens, grid lines 6–8ft apart are about right.

Using an overlay, or a photocopy of your plan complete with grid, mark on the new features that you would like to include, in their approximate positions. You might find it helpful to cut out pieces of paper to an appropriate size and shape so that you can move them around.

Stage 2: the rough

Using an overlay or a photocopy, start sketching in your plan. If you can visualize an overall design, sketch this in first, then move around your features to fit into it. If you have not reached this stage, start by sketching in the features you have provisionally positioned – but be prepared to adjust them as the design evolves.

You will need to make many attempts. Don't be satisfied with the first one – it may be the best, but you won't know this unless you explore other options.

Don't worry about planting details at this stage, except perhaps for a few important plants that form focal points in the design.

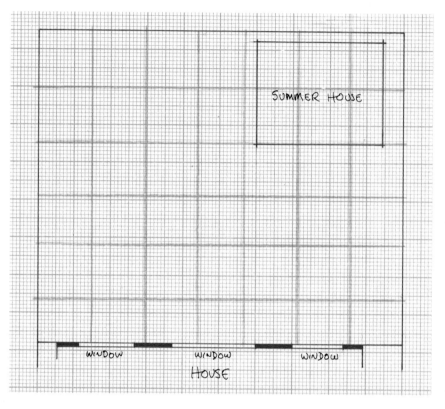

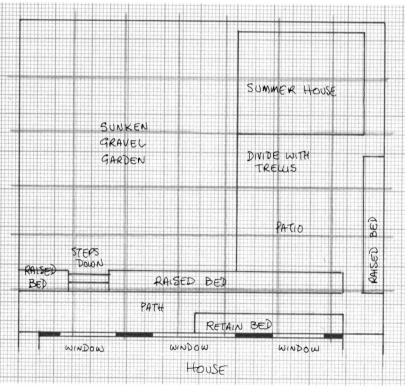

Stage 3: the detailed drawing

Details such as the type of paving should be decided now – not only because it will help you to see the final effect, but also because you need to work to areas that use multiples of full blocks, slabs or bricks if possible. Draw in key plants, especially large trees and shrubs, but omit detailed planting plans at this stage.

Trying it out

Before ordering materials or starting construction, mark out the design in the garden. Use string and pegs to indicate the areas, then walk around them. If possible take a look from an upstairs window. This will give a much better idea of the overall design and whether paths and sitting areas are large enough.

Use tall stakes to indicate the positions of important plants and new trees. This will show how much screening they are likely to offer and whether they may become a problem in time. By observing the shadows cast you will also know whether shade will be a problem – for other plants or for a sitting-out area.

CONSTRUCTION

You can employ a contractor to construct the garden for you, but many gardeners prefer to get help with the main structural features, such as patios and raised beds, and do the rest of the work themselves to keep the cost down. Even the 'heavy' jobs are well within the ability of most gardeners with modest do-it-yourself skills. For more information see the next section.

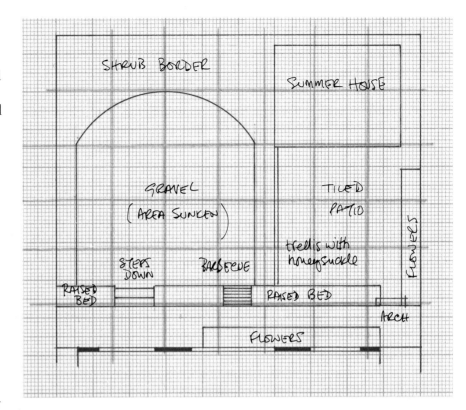

DIFFICULT SITES

Dɪꜰꜰɪᴄᴜʟᴛ sɪᴛᴇs ᴀɴᴅ ᴘʀᴏʙʟᴇᴍ sʜᴀᴘᴇs ᴀʀᴇ ᴀ challenge, but one that can be met with a little determination and a touch of inspiration. Some ways to tackle a selection of special areas are suggested in the following pages.

If your garden is little more than a roof or a balcony, or your house has been wedged in on a building plot that is perhaps L-shaped, or even triangular, traditional garden design techniques might seem difficult to apply.

Many of the design ideas outlined in the previous chapter can still be applied, however, although you may require an alternative design strategy for specific areas.

Patios usually feature as an element in a larger overall design, but in turn have to be designed themselves. Difficult sites like slopes, windy

ᴀʙᴏᴠᴇ: *When your front garden is as tiny as this, compensate by making the most of vertical space with climbers and windowboxes.*

ʟᴇꜰᴛ: *High walls, which would otherwise have dominated this garden, are balanced by strong vertical lines. Even the tops of the walls have been put to good use!*

alleys and passageways between houses demand thoughtful planning and appropriate plants.

Front gardens present a special problem, not because of size or shape, but because a large portion of the garden is usually dedicated to the car – often there is a broad drive to the garage or a hard standing area where the vehicle is left for long periods. Legal restrictions about what you can do with your front garden are another problem – especially on property where the developers or local authority want to maintain an 'open plan' style.

If conditions really are too inhospitable for permanent plants, or the space too limited for a 'proper' garden, containers can provide the answer. Use them creatively, and be prepared to replant or rotate frequently so that they always look good, whatever the time of year.

Unpromising backyards and basements can be transformed as much by a coat of masonry paint, a few choice plants, and some elegant garden furniture and tubs, as by an extensive – and expensive – redesign. Imagination and inspiration are the keynotes for this type of garden design.

In this chapter you will find many solutions to specific problems like these, and even if your particular difficulty is not covered exactly, you should be able to find useful ideas to adapt.

ABOVE: *This long, narrow plot has been broken up into sections, with an angled path so that you don't walk along the garden in a straight line.*

LEFT: *Roof gardens are always cramped, but by keeping most of the pots around the edge it is possible to create a sense of space in the center.*

UNUSUAL SHAPES

Turn a problem shape to your advantage by using its unusual outline to create a garden that stands out from others on your street. What was once a difficult area to fill will soon become the object of other gardeners' envy because of its originality.

Long and narrow – based on a circular theme
This plan shows a design based on a circular theme. The paved area near the house can be used as a patio, and the one at the far end for drying the washing, largely out of sight from the house. Alternatively, if the end of the garden receives more sun, change the roles of the patios.

Taking the connecting path across the garden at an angle, and using small trees or large shrubs to prevent the eye going straight along the sides, creates the impression of a garden to be explored.

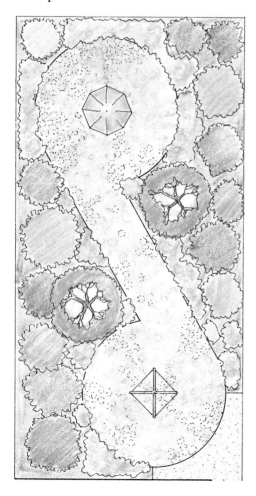

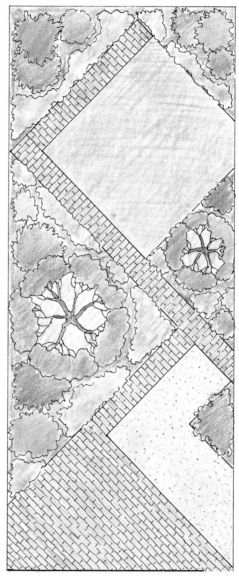

Long and narrow – based on diagonal lines
This garden uses diagonals to divide the garden into sections, but the objective is the same as the circular design. It avoids a straight path from one end of the garden to the other, and brings beds towards the center to produce a series of mini-gardens.

Long and tapered to a point
If the garden is long as well as pointed, consider screening off the main area, leaving a gateway or arch to create the impression of more beyond while not revealing the actual shape. In this plan the narrowing area has been used as an orchard, but it could be a vegetable garden.

Staggering the three paved areas, with small changes of level too, adds interest and prevents the garden looking too long and boring. At the same time, a long view has been retained to give the impression of size.

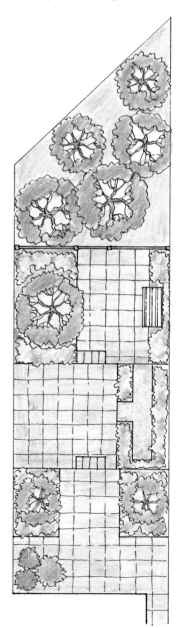

Corner sites

Corner sites are often larger than other plots on the block, and offer scope for some interesting designs. This one has been planned to make the most of the extra space at the side of the house, which has become the main feature rather than the more usual back or front areas.

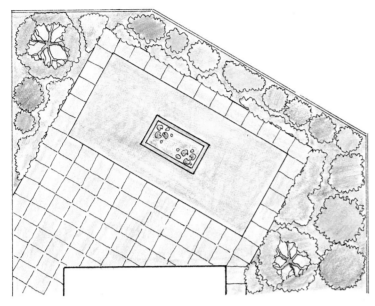

Square and squat

A small square site like this offers little scope for elaborate design, so keep to a few simple elements. To give the impression of greater space the viewpoint has been angled diagonally across the garden. For additional interest, the timber decking is slightly raised, creating a change of level. In a tiny garden a small lawn may be difficult to cut, but you could try an alternative to grass, such as dichondra, which needs mowing only infrequently.

A variety of styles have been used in this plan, in a combination of diagonals and circles – both of which counter the basic rectangle of the garden itself.

Curved corner sites

Curved corner gardens are more difficult to design effectively. In this plan the house is surrounded by a patio on the left-hand side, and a low wall partitions the patio from the rest of the garden, making it more private. For additional interest, the drive is separated from the gravel garden by a path. Gravel and boulders, punctuated by striking plants such as phormiums and yuccas, effectively marry the straight edges with the bold curve created by the corner site.

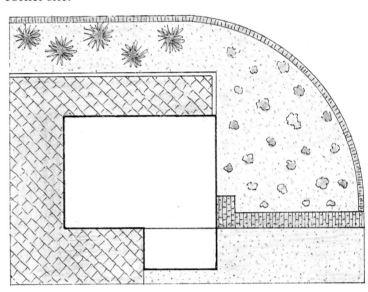

L-shaped

L-shaped gardens offer plenty of scope. Even in a small garden, the opportunity to walk around and explore an area that cannot be seen from one place is a considerable plus-point. This plan shows the clever use of focal points – a tree seat and a seat at the far end – to create a reason to explore the garden. The patio area is partially covered with overhead beams and separated from the rest of the garden by raised flowerbeds.

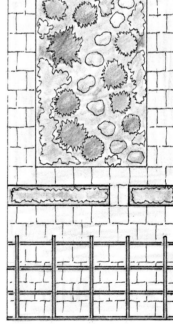

PLANNING PATIOS

The majority of small garden patios are little more than a paved area adjoining the back of the house, usually with little sense of design and often boring for most of the year, yet, with careful designing, your patio can be a key focal point that looks good in all seasons. It should be an attractive feature in its own right yet still form an integrated part of the total garden design.

Siting a patio

The natural choice for a sitting-out area is close to the house, especially if you plan a lot of outdoor eating. It's convenient, and forms an extra 'room', a kind of extension to the home, with a good view of the rest of the garden.

However, this spot may be shady for much of the day, in a wind tunnel created by adjacent buildings, or simply not fit in with your overall garden design.

Be prepared to move the patio away from the main building to gain

ABOVE: *Consider alternatives to paving slabs – bricks, clay and concrete pavers.*
BELOW: *The clever patio overhead makes this area function like an extra room.*

shelter or sun or if it suits your design. Using a position at one side of the garden, or even at the end, may give you more privacy from neighbors or a better view of the garden.

Choosing a shape

Most patios are rectangular – the logical shape for most gardens – but feel free to express yourself in a way that suits the overall design. A circular or semi-circular patio can form part of a circular theme. However, a round patio in a small garden designed around rectangles is likely to look incongruous.

Setting the patio at an angle to the house retains the convenience of straight lines, yet creates a strong sense of design. Consider using this shape on a corner of the house.

Patio boundaries

A clearly defined boundary will emphasize the lines of a design based on a rectangular grid. A low wall, designed with a planting cavity, will soften the hard line between paving and lawn.

High walls should be used with caution as a patio boundary, but occasionally they can be useful on one or perhaps two sides of the patio as a windbreak or privacy screen. A screen block wall will break up the space less than a solid wall, blocks or bricks. Planting suitable shrubs in front of the wall will soften the impact and help to filter the wind.

Changes of level

If the garden slopes towards the house a change of level helps to make a feature of a patio. Use a few shallow

LEFT: *Patios don't have to be by the house. A cosy corner of the garden can even be more appealing.*

BELOW: *A patio at its best where plants and people meet. The use of bricks instead of large slabs gives the illusion of size.*

steps to act like a 'doorway' to the rest of the garden.

A raised patio is a practical solution if your garden slopes away from the house. This creates a vantage point, a terrace from which you can overlook the rest of the garden. On a flat site, simply raising the level by perhaps 6in can be enough to give the patio another dimension.

Paving materials

The choice of paving sets the tone of the patio: brash and colorful, muted but tasteful, integrated or otherwise. Do not be afraid to mix materials: single rows of bricks will break up a large area of slabs. Choose any combination of materials that is appropriate for the setting.

If the patio is close to the house, choose bricks or pavers that match the house bricks closely. The facing bricks used for the house may be unsuitable for paving, but you should be able to achieve a close match.

FINISHING TOUCHES TO PATIO

It is the finishing touches that turn a patio from a hard, flat and uninteresting area into a spot where you can enjoy relaxing.

Patio pergola

The overhead beams of a pergola help to give the patio an enclosed, integrated appearance that effectively extends the home. They provide excellent support for climbers that can bring useful shade as well as beauty. Avoid covering the whole patio with a thick canopy of climbers, however, or you will be searching for the sun, and spattered in drips after a summer shower.

Grape vines are good climbers for an overhead, particularly as their leaves fall so you will get full winter sun. A relative with much larger leaves and gorgeous autumn color is *Vitis coignettiae*.

You can attach overhead beams to a brick wall with joist hangers (remove some of the mortar, insert the hanger, and refill with mortar). Use ground anchors and supports for the posts to keep the timber out of contact with damp ground and prolong its life.

RIGHT: *If you position your patio away from the house, it may be necessary to construct a free-standing overhead feature.*

ABOVE: *Joist hangers are used to secure sawn timber to the house for a patio overhead.*

Built-in features

A built-in barbecue blends with the garden in a way that a free-standing one cannot, and it will probably be used more often. Built-in seats save space and, like the barbecue, give the patio a well-designed look. A few bright cushions give hard bench seats comfort and color.

Planting spaces

Most people pack their patio with containers, but planting directly into the ground makes watering less of a chore. Permanent plants such as shrubs and small trees are best grown in the ground whenever possible. Some manufacturers make paving slabs that are designed to form a series of planting holes.

GETTING THE HEIGHT RIGHT

Patio beams should always be high enough to give plenty of clearance beneath them when clothed with plants. Even plants trained and tied in regularly may have shoots that cascade downwards, and this is especially hazardous with thorny plants such as climbing roses. If the beams are used as hanging basket supports in an area where you will be walking, make sure the bottom of the basket will be above head height. As a guide, a clearance of about 8ft should be the minimum in most instances.

ROOF GARDENS

Despite the handicaps, people manage to create verdant areas on top of buildings. If they are not overlooked, roof gardens can prove to be very private. However, there are potential structural limitations that must be checked out first. Never construct a roof garden without seeking professional advice from a structural engineer on whether the roof is able to take the weight.

You may be advised that your roof is safe, or told to keep the weight to certain areas, perhaps to the parapet wall, but you should abandon any idea of a roof garden if advised that it would be unsafe. Sometimes additional strengthening can be added, but this is a major and potentially expensive job.

Your design will be largely determined by the shape of the roof. Usually raised beds are built in around the edge, with a sitting area in the center. Pots can be used to provide variety within the paved area.

The roof is one place where artificial grass does have a place in the garden. Paving is heavy, artificial grass light. And it adds a touch of much-needed color.

Suitable plants
Most plants simply won't stand the winds and cold winter temperatures on a roof. Choose a framework of wind- and cold-tolerant shrubs, which will provide shelter for the more vulnerable perennial plants and summer bedding flowers.

Windbreak screens
Screens are useful windbreaks but also invaluable in masking many of the unattractive features that a rooftop presents. Use a trellis and cover it with tough climbers such as ivy.

Keeping weight down
Do everything possible to keep down the weight. Avoid thick, heavy paving stones – if you do use paving, choose the thinnest. Use lightweight, loam-free soil mixtures, and plastic or glass-fiber containers instead of terracotta or wood.

ABOVE: *A roof garden can be quite spectacular, especially if the building is strong enough to take structural features like those used here.*
RIGHT: *Trellises provide privacy and shelter from the wind and can be fairly light which avoids increasing the weight.*

Watering
Plants in containers need frequent watering in warm weather. Carrying water to the rooftop in cans soon becomes unappealing, and getting out a hose to connect to a tap indoors can also be cumbersome. Give serious thought to installing an automatic watering system.

FRONT GARDENS

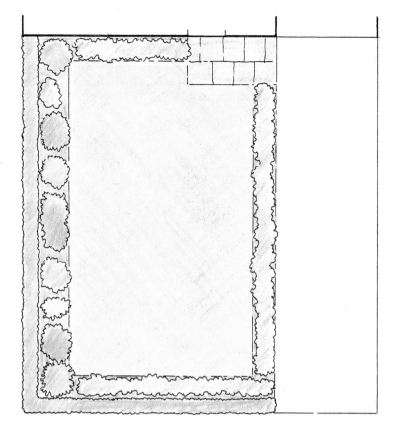

Front gardens greet visitors and can give delight to passers-by. Unfortunately they are difficult to design well if you have to accommodate a driveway for the car, and possibly a separate path to the front door. Even enthusiastic gardeners with delightful back gardens are often let down by an uninspired front garden. We have taken four typical front gardens and shown how they can be improved. Pick ideas from any of these that you think could enhance your own space around the front door.

EXAMPLE ONE

This is a typical design for a front garden: a rectangular lawn is edged with a flower border used mainly for seasonal bedding, and bordered by a hedge. The redesigned garden concentrates on softening the harsh demarcation between drive and ornamental section. Plants now play a more prominent role, and the emphasis is on informality instead of angular lines.

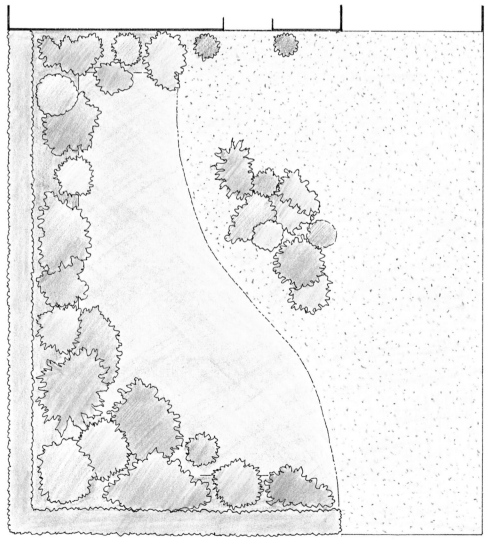

Problems

• The drive isn't part of the garden design, and this makes the area left for plants and grass look even smaller.
• The soil close to the base of a hedge is often dry and impoverished, so bedding plants don't thrive.

Solutions

• Most of the lawn has been dispensed with, and the flower beds enlarged and planted with low-maintenance shrubs. Plenty of evergreens have been used to provide year-round interest.
• Gravel has been used for the drive, and extended to form a broad and informal sweep to the front door. Not everyone likes gravel as a surface to walk on, however, and pavers could have been used instead. If plenty of plants cascade over the edge, the widening sweep would still look soft and attractive.

EXAMPLE TWO

Tall conifers along the drive dominate the garden and will continue to do so even after redesigning it. Remove trees that are too large rather than attempt to design around them.

Problems

● Tall hedges offer privacy, but here the scale is out of proportion, and depending on the aspect may keep out too much light.

● Rose beds are popular, but the small circular bed in the lawn looks incongruous with the rectangular design and can be difficult to mow around.

● Narrow, straight-edged beds around the edges make the lawn seem even smaller.

Solutions

● The concrete drive has been paved with bricks or brick-like pavers.

● A central planting strip has been left to break up the expanse of paving.

● The tall, dark hedge has been replaced with an attractive white ranch fence. The gravelled area beneath is planted with alpines.

● Climbing roses replace the central weeping rose. Trained against the house they provide a fragrant welcome in summer.

● Existing borders remain to minimize the reconstruction.

● Small shrubs such as hebes and lavenders have been used, along with low-growing perennials like *Stachys lanata* (syn. *S. byzantina* or *S. olympica*) and *Bergenia cordifolia*, instead of seasonal bedding plants.

● A small deciduous tree, a crab apple, replaces the large conifer in the bottom corner. The area beneath can be planted with spring-flowering bulbs such as crocuses and snowdrops.

● The small circular bed has been enlarged and filled with gravel, as a base on which to stand pots.

● The narrow bed has been filled in with grass removed when the new paving in front of the house was laid. Bricks or blocks form a crisp edge.

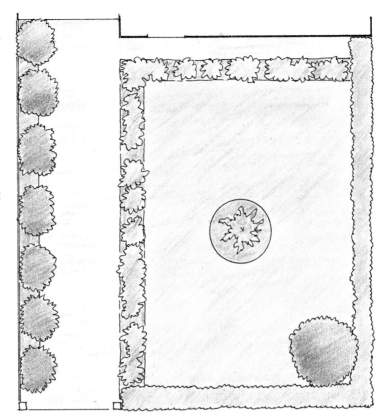

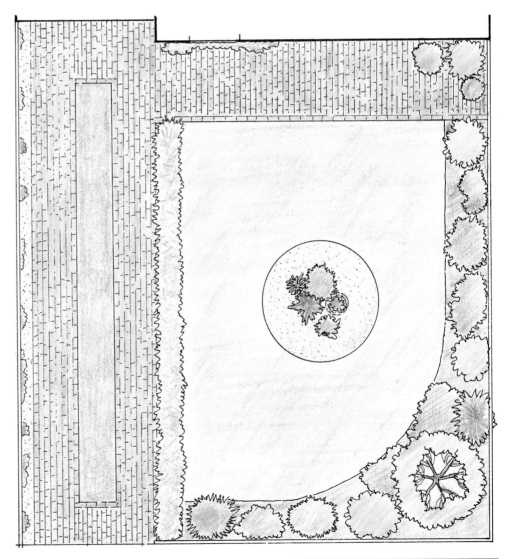

FRONT GARDENS

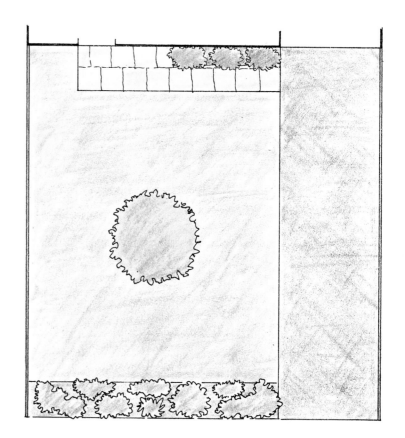

EXAMPLE THREE

Gardens don't come much more boring than this: a concrete drive, small narrow flower bed in front of the window and along the edge of the garden, and a single flowering cherry tree.

The solution for this garden was a simple one, as the redesigned garden shows. The cottage-garden style includes plants of all kinds which grow and mingle happily together with minimum intervention.

Besides being a short cut to the front door, the stepping stones encourage exploration of the garden and its plants. You actually walk through the planting, which cascades and tumbles around the paving slabs. The garden design has been reversed, with plants forming the heart of the garden rather than peripherals around the edge.

Problems

● Although the cherry is spectacular in flower, and provides a show of autumn color, it is only attractive for a few weeks of the year. Its present position precludes any major redesign and so it is best removed.
● Unclothed wooden fences add to the drab appearance.
● Small flower beds like these lack impact, and are too small for the imaginative use of shrubs or herbaceous perennials.

Solutions

● The lawn and tree have been removed, and the whole area planted with a mixture of dwarf shrubs, herbaceous perennials, hardy annuals, and lots of bulbs for spring interest.
● Stepping-stones have been provided for those who want to take a short-cut (they also make access for weeding easier).
● The fences have been replaced with low walls so that the garden seems less confined.

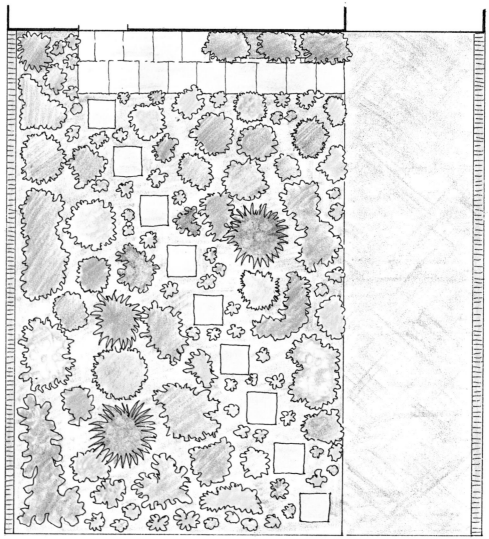

EXAMPLE FOUR

This garden is a jumble of shapes and angles, and lacks any sense of design. With its new look, the old curved path has been retained because its thick concrete base and the drain inspection covers within it would have made it difficult to move, but all the other lines have been simplified and more appropriate plants used.

Problems

● Rock gardens are seldom successful on a flat site, and although small rock beds in a lawn can be made to resemble a natural rock outcrop, in this position the rocks can never look convincing.

● The tree here is young but will grow large and eventually cast considerable shade and dominate the garden.

● Small beds like this, used for seasonal bedding, are colorful in summer but can lack interest in winter. This curve sits uneasily with the straight edge at one end and the curve of the path at the other.

Solutions

● The rock garden has been paved so that the cultivated area is not separated by the drive.

● Gravel replaces the lawn. This needs minimal maintenance and acts as a good foil for the plants.

● Dwarf and medium-sized conifers create height and cover. By using species and varieties in many shades of green and gold, and choosing a range of shapes, this part of the garden now looks interesting throughout the year.

● Stepping-stones add further interest. Because it isn't possible to see where the stepping stones lead to from either end (the conifers hide the route), a sense of mystery is added and this tempts the visitor to explore.

● The existing path has been retained, but covered with slate crazy-paving it looks more interesting.

● A pond creates a water feature.

● The awkward, narrow curving strip has been turned into a 'stream', with circulating water flowing over a cascade into the pond at one end.

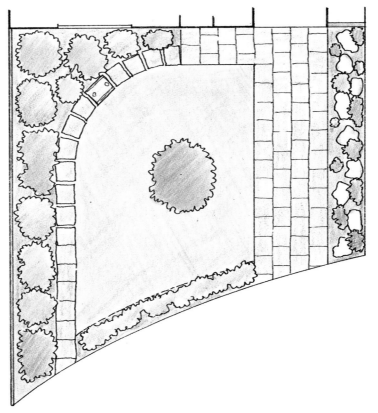

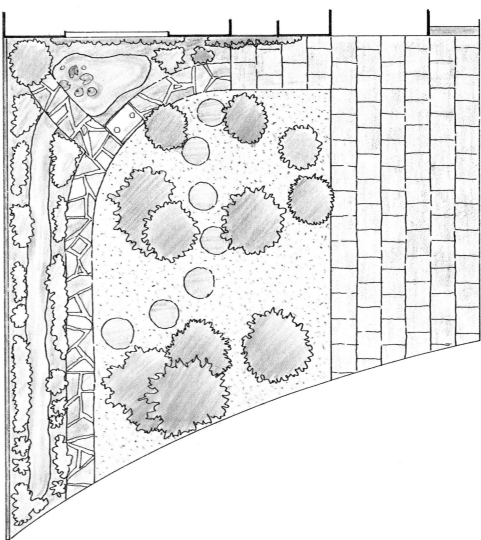

BASEMENT GARDENS AND BACKYARDS

Some gardens are not just small, they are gloomy too because they are below street level, or hemmed in by tall walls. Because there is little that can be done to alter this sort of garden structurally, it is best to direct any efforts towards improving the environment and devising a strategy that helps plants survive, or at least ensure lots of lush-looking plants to flourish despite the handicaps. Not all of the techniques shown here will be applicable to your own garden, but most of them can be adapted to suit even the most unpromising site.

Using lighting

Garden lights can extend the hours of enjoyment you derive from your garden, and you don't need many of them for a lot of impact in a small area. You can illuminate most of the space – useful if you often entertain in the evening – or use just one or two spotlights to pick out dramatic elements in the design. Some can be swivelled so that you can highlight different features. For subtle lighting, a cheaper and pretty option is to use lanterns which hold candles.

Painting the walls

In a garden enclosed by walls or fences, you need to do everything possible to reflect light and make the background bright and cheerful. Painting the walls a pale color will improve things dramatically.

Using trellis

Trellis can be used as a decorative feature in its own right, or as a plant support. If you want to make a feature of it, paint it white, but if it is used primarily as a plant support, make sure it has been treated with a non-toxic preservative. Enclose unsightly drainpipes in a trellis 'box' over which you can grow an evergreen climber such as ivy.

Adding water features

The sound of running water is refreshing on a summer's day, and in a small area you need only a trickle to do the job. A wall spout (with a tiny pool at ground level, from which the

ABOVE: *Ferns thrive in shady positions where many other plants would languish. If you can provide moisture from a water feature, so much the better.*
RIGHT: *Even the tiniest basement garden or backyard has space for a water feature.*

water is recirculated) or a self-contained wall fountain is ideal.

Introducing wind chimes

Wind chimes both look and sound good. Choose one primarily for the sound it makes.

Training wall shrubs

Cover some of the walls with climbers, but try espalier or fan-trained fruit trees or espalier pyracanthas too.

Furnishing in style

White-painted furniture looks bright in a small, enclosed garden, but don't add too much furniture or the area will look cluttered rather than elegant.

Using containers with character

If the area is small, make everything work for its space. Instead of plastic containers, use interesting old kitchen utensils, or other unexpected holders, but be sure to add drainage holes to prevent waterlogging.

Focal points in shade

Basement areas and enclosed backyards are often inhospitable for plants – the light is poor and the walls keep off much of the rain. If, in addition, you have a tree that casts shade, even the shade-loving plants will struggle. Use these positions for ornaments or make them into focal points.

Planting ferns

Ferns do well in a cool, shady spot, so use them freely in those areas too dull for bright summer flowers. Try a collection of hardy ferns – they won't look dull if you nestle an attractive ornament among them, or include white flowers, perhaps backed by a white wall. On a hot summer's day the space will be an oasis of coolness and tranquility.

Growing white-flowered plants

Use pale flowers if the area lacks direct sun. You won't be able to use plants that need strong sun light, but fortunately some of the best white-flowering plants are shade-tolerant. Try white varieties of impatiens and white nicotianas, for example. White flowers will show up more brilliantly than colored ones in a dull spot.

Introducing exotics

Gardens enclosed by walls can be hot and sunny too, and being sheltered provides the ideal environment for many exotic plants to grow successfully. Try a few bold houseplants to create a tropical effect.

LEFT: *Use wall pots and half baskets to make a dominant wall more interesting. They will be more effective staggered rather than in straight rows.*

LEFT BELOW: *White flowers, like this nicotiana, show up well in darker corners.*

Making the most of steps

Open railings can be used as supports for attractive climbers, planted in pots at the base of the steps, but always keep them trimmed so that slippery leaves do not trail across the steps or obstruct the hand-rail. If the steps are very wide, place pots of bright flowers on the steps themselves to produce a ribbon of color. Do not obstruct the steps. If there is no space on the steps, use a group of containers filled with flowers at the top and bottom of the stairway.

Fixing windowboxes and wall baskets

Use windowboxes lavishly – not only beneath windows but fixed to walls too. Windowboxes, wall pots and half-baskets can all bring cascades of color to a bare wall. Stagger the rows instead of placing them in neat and tidy lines.

Capturing the scents

An enclosed garden is an ideal place in which to grow scented plants – the fragrances are held in the air instead of being carried off on the wind. Use plenty of aromatic plants, especially big and bold plants like daturas, and those with a heavy perfume such as evening-scented nicotianas and night-scented stocks.

BALCONIES AND VERANDAS

For someone without a garden, a balcony may be their entire 'outdoor room', and a 'garden' to enjoy from indoors when the weather is inclement. Even more than a patio, the balcony or veranda is an outdoor extension of the home.

The area is usually small, so the money you are prepared to spend on gardening will go a long way. Invest in high quality flooring and furniture, and ornate containers, which will create a classy setting for your plants.

Choosing flooring

The floor will help to set the tone and style, and it can make or mar a tiny 'garden' like this.

Paving slabs are best avoided: they are heavy, frequently lack the kind of refinement that you can achieve with tiles, and the size of individual slabs may be too large to look 'in scale' for the small area being covered.

Think of the veranda or balcony floor as you might the kitchen or conservatory floor – and use materials that you might use indoors. Quarry tiles and decorative ceramic tiles work well, and produce a good visual link with the house. Make sure ceramic tiles are frostproof however. Tiles are relatively light in weight, and their small size is in proportion to the area.

Wooden decking is another good choice for a veranda.

The problem of aspect

Aspect is an important consideration. Unlike a usual garden, or even a roof garden, the light may be strong and intense all day, or there may be constant shade, depending on position. Balconies above may also cast shade.

If the aspect is sunny, some shade from above can be helpful. Consider installing an adjustable awning that you can pull down to provide shade for a hot spot. Choose sun-loving plants adapted to dry conditions for this situation – your indoor cacti and

RIGHT: *Roof gardens and balconies are often improved if you lay a wooden floor and create a lattice overhead.*

succulents will be happy to go outside for the summer.

If the aspect is shady for most of the day a lot of flowering plants won't thrive. You may have to concentrate on foliage plants, though some bright flowers, such as impatiens and nicotiana, do well in shade.

Countering the wind

Like roof gardens, balconies are often exposed to cold and damaging winds. The higher a balcony the greater problem wind is likely to be.

To grow tender and exotic plants, provide a screen that will filter the wind without causing turbulent eddies. A trellis clothed with a tough evergreen such as an ivy is useful, or use screens of woven bamboo or reeds on the windiest side – these not only provide useful shelter and privacy, but make an áttractive backdrop for plants in containers.

Adding color round the year

Create a framework of tough evergreens to clothe the balcony or veranda throughout the year, and provide a backdrop for the more colorful seasonal flowers.

Use plenty of bright seasonal flowers in windowboxes or troughs along the edge, with trailers that cascade down over the edge.

In the more sheltered positions, grow lots of exotic-looking plants, and don't be afraid to give lots of your tough-leaved houseplants a summer holiday outside.

Pots of spring-flowering bulbs extend the season of bright flowers, but choose compact varieties – tall daffodils, for example, will almost certainly be bent forward as wind bounces back off the walls.

Add splashes of color with cut flowers. In summer choose long-lasting 'exotics' such as strelitzias and anthuriums.

ABOVE: *In mild areas or a sheltered position, you can turn your balcony into a tropical garden.*

RIGHT: *Turn your balcony into an outdoor room where many indoor plants thrive in summer.*

FEATURES
and STRUCTURES

Overall garden design is important, but it is individual features that make a garden special. Major structural decisions, such as the type of paving to use, the shape of the lawn, or how to define the boundaries, have a significant impact, but even small details like ornaments and garden lights can lift a small garden above the ordinary. The use of containers is especially important in a small garden — on a tiny balcony they may be the garden. Use them imaginatively, choosing containers that are decorative, and grouping them for added interest.

ABOVE: *Create the urge to explore with small paths that lead to features such as seats and ornaments.*

OPPOSITE: *The garden floor is important, whether paving or a lawn, but it is features, like this arbor and its seat, that give the garden character.*

the GARDEN FLOOR

THE GARDEN FLOOR – LAWN, PAVING, PATHS, even areas of gravel or ground cover plants – can make or mar your garden. These surfaces are likely to account for more area than the beds and borders. Although they recede in importance when the garden is in full bloom, for much of the year they probably hold center stage.

Removing existing paths and paved areas presents a practical problem. If they are laid on a thick bed of concrete you will probably have to rent equipment to break up the surface. Provided these areas do not compromise your design too much, it is much easier to leave as many as you can in position. Consider paving over the top with a more sympathetic material. It should be relatively easy to extend the area if you want to.

Lawns are more easily modified than paths and paved areas. At worst you can dig them up and resow or relay them. If you simply want to change the shape, you can trim off surplus grass or lift and relay just part of the lawn.

ABOVE: *Paths can be both functional and attractive, often giving the garden shape and form.*

OPPOSITE: *The combination of hard landscaping, such as bricks, with soft landscaping, such as lawns, can look very harmonious if designed with integration in mind.*

OPPOSITE ABOVE: *A brick edging marks the boundary between lawn and border, and serves the practical purpose of making mowing easier.*

LEFT: *Areas like this would soon become weedy if not densely planted. Here hostas suppress the weeds, and Soleirolia soleirolii spills over onto the path.*

Wooden decking is very popular in some countries, seldom used in others. Much depends on the price of wood locally, and to some extent the climate, but decking should always be on your list of options.

There are useful alternatives to grass for areas that are not used for recreation or are seldom trodden on. Ground cover plants not only suppress weeds in flower beds, but can replace a lawn where the surface does not have to take the wear and tear of trampling feet. Inset stepping-stones to protect the plants. Where the garden is *very* small, low-growing ground cover may be much more practical than a lawn that is almost too tiny to cut with a mower.

LAWNS

The lawn is often the centerpiece of a small garden, the canvas against which the rest of the garden is painted. For many gardeners this makes it worth all the mowing, feeding and grooming that a good lawn demands. If your lawn has to serve as a play area too, be realistic and sow tough grasses, and settle for a hard-wearing lawn rather than a showpiece. It can still look green and lush – the important consideration from a design viewpoint. Instead of aiming for a putting-green finish, the shape of the lawn or a striking edging could be its strong visual message.

Working with circles

Circular lawns can be very effective. Several circular lawns, linked by areas of paving, such as cobbles, work well in a long, narrow garden.

If the garden is very small, all you will have space for is a single circular lawn. If you make it the centerpoint with beds around it that become deeper towards the corner of the garden, you will be able to combine small trees and tall shrubs at the back with smaller shrubs and herbaceous plants in front. To add interest, include a couple of stepping-stone paths that lead to a hidden corner.

Using rectangles

Rectangular lawns can look boring, but sometimes they can be made more interesting by extending another garden feature – such as a patio or flower bed – into them to produce an L-shaped lawn.

Alternatively, include an interesting feature such as a birdbath or sundial (often better towards one side or end of the lawn than in the middle). A water feature is another good way to break up a boring rectangle of grass.

An angled lawn

If you have chosen a diagonal theme for your design, you will probably want to set your lawn at an angle to the house so that it fits in with the

ABOVE RIGHT: *A sweeping lawn can help to create a sense of perspective.*
RIGHT: *This lawn would look boring with straight edges – the curves add style.*

other features. The same rectangle of lawn becomes much more interesting when set at an angle of about 45 degrees. By lifting and patching the lawn, you may be able to achieve this without having to start from scratch.

Creating curves

A sweeping lawn with bays and curves where the flower borders ebb and flow is very attractive. It is difficult to achieve in a small garden. However, you can bring out a border in a large curve so the grass disappears around the back. You may be able to do this by extending the border into an existing rectangular lawn.

Changing height

If you have to create an impression in a small space, try a raised or sunken lawn. The step does not have to be large – 6–9in is often enough. If making a sunken lawn, always include a mowing edge so that you can use the mower right up to the edge of the grass.

ABOVE: *Sunken lawns make a bold feature.*

KEEPING A TRIM EDGE

Circular lawns must be edged properly. Nothing looks worse than a circle that isn't circular, and of course constant trimming back will eat into the lawn over the years. To avoid this, incorporate a firm edging, such as bricks placed on end and mortared into position, when you make the lawn.

Where the edges are straight use proprietary lawn edging strips.

HOW TO CREATE A MOWING EDGE

If flowers tumble out of your borders, or there is a steep edge that makes mowing difficult, lay a mowing edge of bricks or paving slabs.

1 Mark out the area of grass to be lifted using the paving as a guide. Lift the grass where you want to lay the paved edge. To keep the new edge straight, use a half-moon edger against the paving slab. Then lift the grass to be removed by slicing it off with a spade.

2 Make a firm base by compacting gravel or a mixture of sand and gravel where the paving is to be laid. Use a plank of wood to ensure it is level. Allow for the thickness of the paving and a few blobs of mortar.

3 It is best to bed the edging on mortar for stability, but as it will not be taking a heavy weight just press the slabs onto blobs of mortar and tap level (use a spirit-level to double-check).

GRASS SUBSTITUTES

Grass is still the best form of living carpet for a large lawn subject to wear, but small areas are ideal for experimenting with those alternatives to grass that will give your garden a highly individual touch.

RIGHT: *For an attractive-looking lawn in a small area not subject to heavy wear, chamomile is ideal.*

BELOW: *Thyme is tough enough to grow between paving, where it is often crushed underfoot.*

None of the plants described will form such a hard-wearing lawn as grass, but they have their own attractions. Bear in mind that you can't use a normal selective lawn weedkiller on these broad-leaved plants, so be prepared for some hand weeding. On a small-scale, however, this is manageable, and a price worth paying if you fancy a lawn with a difference.

Scent with chamomile

This classic grass substitute has been used for centuries to make an attractive, pale green lawn. Its lovely aroma when walked on, combined with an ability to tolerate a reasonable amount of wear, makes it an excellent choice for a small, ornamental area. But, like the other plants suggested here, chamomile is not a practical proposition for a children's play area.

What it looks like Chamomile has small, feathery, aromatic leaves and white daisy flowers, though the non-flowering 'Treneague' is preferable, as flowers spoil the close carpeted effect. It spreads rapidly by creeping stems, which is one reason why it makes such a good substitute for grass.

How to sow or plant You can sow seed, but the best lawns are established from young offshoots or cuttings of a non-flowering variety. If you buy seed, start them off in seed trays to produce young plants to put out later. If you buy young plants or offshoots by post they will probably arrive in a plastic bag – larger specimens from a garden center will

be pot-grown but you will pay more.

Plant 9in apart – closer if you have a lot of seed-raised plants or cuttings of your own. Close spacing will achieve quicker cover, but the final result is unlikely to be any better. If you are growing from seed, start off under glass in early spring, and plant out in late spring, rather than sowing directly in the open ground like grass.

Trim with the mower set high to encourage the development of sideshoots if the plants do not seem to be making enough bushy side growth. You will have to mow flowering forms occasionally to keep the plants compact.

You may find chamomile under one of its two widely used Latin names *Chamaemelum nobile* or *Anthemis nobilis*.

Thyme

Thyme is another popular alternative to grass for a small area, but be sure to choose the right kind of thyme. The culinary species is too tall and bushy for this purpose. Choose the more prostrate *Thymus serpyllum*.

Thymes are good for dry soils, and do well in alkaline (limey) areas. Unfortunately they tend to become woody and straggly after about four or five years. Cuttings are easy to root, however, so periodic replanting should not be an expensive task.

What it looks like Thymes have small, aromatic leaves, and *T. serpyllum* has low, spreading growth 2in high. Clusters of tiny purple, white, pink, red, or lavender flowers appear in summer.

How to sow or plant Plant about 9in apart. You can raise your own plants from seed (sow in trays, not directly into the soil).

HOW TO PLANT A THYME LAWN

1 Prepare the ground thoroughly by digging over the area and leveling it at least a month before planting. Dig out any weeds that appear. Hoe off seedlings. Rake level.

2 Water the plants in their pots, then set them out about 8in apart, in staggered rows (a little closer for quicker cover, a little further apart for economy but slower cover).

3 Knock the plant from its pot and carefully tease out a few of the roots if they are running tightly around the edge of the pot.

5 Water the ground thoroughly and keep well watered for the first season.

4 Plant at their original depth, and firm the soil around the roots before planting the next one.

ABOVE: *Clover – in this case wild white – makes a novel lawn, as gardeners usually spend so much time trying to eliminate it.*

Clover

If clovers seem to thrive better than the grass in your existing lawn, eliminate the grass and try a clover lawn – it will probably look greener than grass in dry weather! You will, of course, still have to weed, to remove non-clover seedlings.

What it looks like The three-lobed leaves of the clover are well known. The white or purple flowers should not be a feature of a clover lawn – mow the plants before they are tall enough to flower.

How to sow or plant Clover is sown in-situ, on ground cleared of weeds, ideally in spring. You can sometimes buy clover seed from companies specializing in wild flower seeds. White clover (*Trifolium repens*) is a good one to sow for a lawn.

Cotula

There are several low-growing species of cotula that can be used for a lawn. In some countries they are regarded as lawn weeds, in others lawns are sometimes created for them. They are worth a try if you are prepared for a rampant plant that may need curtailing.

What it looks like Cotulas are low-growing plants, with divided, fern-like leaves. The creeping stems root as they grow. Masses of small yellow flowers are produced in mid summer.

How to sow or plant Plant about 4–6in apart. *Cotula coronopifolia* is the one usually used as a grass substitute. The cheapest way is to sow seed, but this is only likely to be available from suppliers dealing in the less common plants.

IMAGINATIVE PAVING

Most small gardens have a patio or at least a paved area close to the house. Often it is the main feature around which the remainder of the back garden is arranged. It can be the link that integrates home and garden. At its worst, paving can be boring and off-putting; at its best it can make a real contribution to the overall impact of the garden.

On the following pages you will find a selection of popular paving materials, with suggestions for use, and their advantanges and disadvantages. Always shop around because the availability and price of natural stones vary enormously, not only from country to country, but also from area to area.

Even the availability of man-made paving will vary from one area to another. Choosing the material is only part of the secret of successful paving – how you use it, alone or combined with other materials, is what can make an area of paving mundane or something special.

Color combinations
Your liking for bright and brash color combinations will depend on the effect you want to create. Be wary of bright colors though – they can detract from the plants, although they will mellow with age.

Sizing up the problem
In a small garden, large-sized paving units can destroy the sense of scale. Try small-sized paving slabs (which are also easier to handle), or go for bricks, pavers, or cobbles.

Mix and match
Mixing different paving materials can work well, even in a small space. Try areas or rows of bricks or clay pavers with paving slabs, railway sleepers with bricks, in fact any combination that looks good together and blends with the setting. Avoid using more than three different materials, however, as this can look too fussy in a small garden.

LEFT: *Bricks and pavers often look more attractive if laid to a pattern such as this herringbone style.*

Paving patterns
You can go for a completely random pattern – crazy-paving is a perfect example – but most paving is laid to a pre-planned pattern using rectangular paving slabs or bricks. Look at the brochures for paving slabs. These usually suggest a variety of ways in which the slabs can be laid.

Although a large area laid with slabs of the same size can look boring, avoid too many different sizes, or complex patterns in a small space. Simplicity is often more effective.

Bricks and clay pavers are often the best choice for a small area, because their small size is more likely to be in harmony with the scale of the garden. The way they are laid makes a significant visual difference, however, so choose carefully.

The stretcher bond is usually most effective for a small area, and for paths. The herringbone pattern is suitable for both large and small areas, but the basket weave needs a reasonably large expanse for the pattern to be appreciated.

Stretcher bond

Herringbone

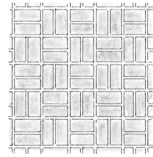

Basket weave

HOW TO LAY PAVING

1 Excavate the area to a depth that will allow for about 2in of compacted hardcore topped with about 1–2in of ballast, plus the thickness of the paving and mortar. As an alternative to hardcore topped with ballast, you can use 2in of scalpings. Check the depth of the foundation before laying the paving. If adjoining the house, make sure that the paving will end up below the damp-proof course.

2 Put five blobs of mortar where the slab is to be placed – one at each corner, and the other in the middle.

3 Alternatively, cover the area where the paving is to be laid with mortar, then level.

4 Position the slab carefully, bedding it on the mortar.

5 Use a spirit-level to ensure that the slab is level, but use a small wedge of wood under one end to create a slight slope over a large area of paving so that rainwater runs off freely. Tap the slab down further, or raise it by lifting and packing in a little more mortar. Position the level over more than one slab (place it on a straight-edged piece of wood if necessary).

6 Use spacers of an even thickness to ensure regular spacing. Remove these later, before the joints are filled with mortar.

7 A day or two after laying the paving, go over it again to fill in the joints. Use a small pointing trowel and a dryish mortar mix to do this. Finish off with a smooth stroke that leaves the mortar slightly recessed. This produces an attractive, crisp look. Wash any surplus mortar off the slabs before it dries.

PAVING MATERIALS

There are plenty of paving materials from which to choose, so spend time looking through brochures and visit garden centers and builders' merchants before you come to a decision.

RIGHT: *Bricks, unlike clay pavers, are laid with mortared joints. This can emphasize the design.*

PAVING SLABS
Rectangular paving slabs

The majority of paving slabs are based on a full-sized slab, usually either 18 × 18in or 18 × 24in. Half and quarter slabs may be a little smaller in proportion to allow for mortar joints. Thickness may vary according to make but, provided you mix only those made by the same manufacturer, this won't matter.

A *smooth* surface can be boring, slippery, and a little too much like public paving, but many have a *textured* finish. Textures vary: a riven finish usually looks like natural stone, an exposed aggregate finish has exposed gravel to give a natural-looking non-slip finish.

Slabs imprinted with a section of a larger pattern are usually unsatisfactory in a small area. As quite a large area of paving is usually required to complete the pattern, they only emphasize the space limitations.

Shaped paving slabs

Use shaped slabs with caution. Circular slabs are useful for stepping-stones, but are difficult to design into a small patio. Hexagonal slabs also need a fairly large area to be appreciated. Special half-block edging pieces are usually available to produce a straight edge.

Paved and cobbled finish slabs

Some designs are stamped with an impression to resemble groups of pavers or bricks, some containing as many as eight basket-weave 'bricks' within the one slab. They create the illusion of smaller paving units, and are very effective in a small area.

TOP LEFT: *Slabs like this are particularly useful for a small area because they give the illusion of smaller paving units.*
TOP RIGHT: *Paving slabs with a riven finish look convincingly like real weathered stone.*
MIDDLE LEFT: *Paving slabs will always weather. Pale colors like this will soon look darker, while bright colors will become more muted.*
MIDDLE RIGHT: *Hexagonal paving slabs can be attractive, but are not usually satisfactory in a very small area.*
BOTTOM: *Rectangular shapes like this can be used alone, or integrated with other sizes to build up an attractive design.*

Planting circles

A few manufacturers produce paving slabs with an arc taken out of one corner. Four of these placed together leave a circular planting area for a tree or other specimen plant.

BRICKS AND PAVERS

Bricks and pavers are especially useful for a small garden. You can create an attractive design even in a small area, and you may be able to obtain them in a color and finish that matches your home, which will produce a more integrated effect.

Always check that the bricks are suitable for paving, however, as some intended for house building will not withstand the frequent saturation and freezing that paths and patios are subjected to. After a few seasons they will begin to crumble. Clay pavers, on the other hand, have been fired in a way that makes them suitable for paving. Concrete pavers and blocks are another option, though these are usually more suitable for a drive than a small patio.

Rectangular pavers

Clay pavers look superficially like bricks but are designed to lock together without mortar. They are also thinner than most bricks, though this is not obvious once they have been laid. Concrete pavers or paving blocks are laid in a similar way and are more attractive than concrete laid in-situ for a drive. They can look a little 'municipal'.

Interlocking pavers and blocks

Concrete pavers or blocks are often shaped so that they interlock. Interlocking clay pavers may also be available.

Bricks

Bricks require mortar joints – they won't interlock snugly like clay pavers. On the other hand you may be able to use the same bricks for raised beds and low walls, giving the whole design a more planned and well-integrated appearance.

To use bricks economically, lay them with their largest surface exposed, not on edge. This excludes the use of pierced bricks (which have holes through them). It does not matter if they have a frog (depression) on one side, provided this is placed face-down.

Setts and cobbles

Imitation granite setts, which are made from reconstituted stone, and cobbles, which are natural, large, rounded stones shaped by the sea or glaciers, are both excellent for small areas of irregular shape. Their size makes them much easier to lay to a curve. Bed them into a mortar mix on a firm base.

Tiles

Quarry and ceramic tiles are appropriate for small areas near the house, or to create a patio that looks just that little bit different. Always make sure ceramic tiles are frostproof. Lay them on a concrete base that has been allowed to set, and fix them with an adhesive recommended by the supplier or manufacturer.

LEFT: *Hard paving comes in many forms. The top row shows (from left to right) natural stone sett, clay paver, clay brick, artificial sett. The center row shows a typical range of concrete paving blocks. The bottom row illustrates some of the colors available in concrete paving slabs.*

PATHS AND PATH MATERIALS

As with any other garden structure, paths should be designed to suit the purpose they are to serve. There is a wide range of materials on the market to suit every need, so shop around before deciding which you require.

Practical paths should be functional first and attractive second. Drives for cars and paths to the front door must be firmly laid on proper foundations. And don't skimp on width – it is extremely frustrating for visitors if they have to approach your door in single file. It might be better for the route to take a detour, perhaps forming an L-shape with the drive, if there isn't enough space for a wide path directly to the door.

Internal paths, used to connect one part of the garden to another, can be more lightly constructed, and are softened with plants.

Casual paths, which often lead nowhere and are created for effect, such as stepping-stones through a flower bed, can be lightly constructed and much less formal in style.

RIGHT: *Although the gaps between these paving slabs have been filled with chipped bark in this example, you could also use gravel.*

BELOW: *Paving can reflect artistic ambitions.*
BELOW RIGHT: *Victorian-style rope edging.*

Bricks and pavers
These are ideal materials for internal garden paths that have to be both practical and pretty. Complex bonding patterns are best avoided unless the path is very wide.

Paving slabs
By mixing them with other materials the look of paving slabs can be much improved. A narrow gravel strip either side can look smart, and the gravel can be extended between the joints to space out the slabs. The slab-and-gravel combination is ideal if you need a curved path.

A straight path can be broken up with strips of beach pebbles mortared between the slabs. Tamp them in so that they are flush with the surrounding paving.

Crazy-paving

Use this with caution. In the right place, and using a natural stone, the effect can be mellow, and harmonize well with the plants. Be more wary of using broken paving slabs – even though they are cheap. Colored ones can look garish, and even neutral slabs still look angular and lack the softness of natural stone.

Path edgings

Paths always make a smarter feature with a neat or interesting edging. If you have an older-style property, try a Victorian-style edging. If it is a country cottage, try something both subtle and unusual, like green glass bottles sunk into the ground so that just the bottoms are visible. Or use bricks: on their sides, on end, or set at an angle of about 45 degrees.

CREVICE PLANTS

Plants look attractive and soften the harsh outline of a rigid or straight path. They are easy to use with crazy-paving or any path edged with gravel. It may be necessary to excavate small holes. Fill them with a good potting mixture. Sow or plant into these prepared pockets.

Some of the best plants to use for areas likely to be trodden on are chamomile, *Thymus serpyllum* and *Cotula squalida*. For areas not likely to be trodden on there are many more good candidates, such as *Ajuga reptans* and *Armeria maritima*.

HOW TO LAY CLAY OR CONCRETE PAVERS

The method of laying clay or concrete pavers described in the following steps can be used for a drive or a patio as well as a path.

1 Excavate the area and prepare a sub-base of about 2in of compacted hardcore or sand and gravel mix. Set an edging along one end and side first, mortaring into position, before laying the pavers.

2 Lay a 2in bed of sharp sand over the area, then use a straight-edged piece of wood stretched between two height gauges (battens fixed at the height of the sand bed) to strike off surplus sand and provide a level surface.

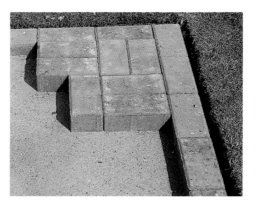

3 Position the pavers, laying approximately 6½ft at a time. Make sure they butt up to each other, and are firm against the edging. Mortar further edging strips into place as you proceed.

4 Rent a flat-plate vibrator to consolidate the sand. Alternatively, tamp the pavers down with a club hammer over a piece of wood. Do not go too close to an unsupported edge with the vibrator.

5 Brush more sand into the joints, then vibrate or tamp again. It may be necessary to repeat this once more.

WOODEN DECKING

Wooden decking creates a distinctive effect, and will make a refreshing change from ordinary paving for the patio area. As with paving, the material used should be in proportion to the size of the garden, so the width of the planks is important. Wide planks look best in a large garden, but in a small, enclosed area narrower planks are usually preferable.

Different designs can be achieved by using planks of different widths and fixing them in different directions, as illustrated here, but on the whole it is best to keep any pattern fairly simple. Leave a small gap between each plank, but not so large that high-heeled shoes can slip into it.

The construction method and wood sizes must reflect the size of the overall structure and its design – especially if built up over sloping ground. In some countries there are building codes and regulations that may have to be met. If in doubt, seek professional help with the design, even if you construct it yourself.

All wood used for decking must be thoroughly treated with a wood preservative. Some preservatives and wood stains are available in a range of colors, and this provides the opportunity for a little creativity. Dark browns and black always look good and weather well, but if you want to be more adventurous choose from reds, greens and grays.

If you want your decking to have a long life, special pressure-treated timber is the best choice. However, the range of colors available is bound to be less extensive.

Parquet decking

The easiest way to use wood as a surface is to make or buy parquet decking. Provided the ground is flat panels are easy to lay and can look very pleasing. Bed them on about 2in of sand over a layer of gravel, to ensure free drainage beneath. If you already have a suitable concrete base to use, you can lay them directly onto this.

LEFT: *Wooden decking makes a refreshing change from paving slabs or bricks, and can give the garden a touch of class.*

Patterns of wooden decking

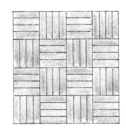
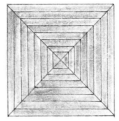

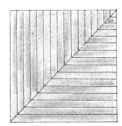

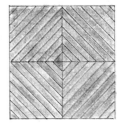
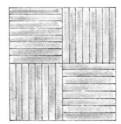
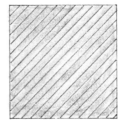

GROUND COVER WITH PLANTS

If you want to cover an area of ground with a living carpet simply for texture, and don't expect to walk on the area, suitable ground cover plants are the answer.

To use ground cover plants like this, rather than simply as a means to suppress weeds in a flower bed, they must be evergreen, compact, and grow to a low, even height.

HOW TO PLANT CLUMP-FORMING GROUND COVER

1 Clear the ground of weeds first, and be especially careful to remove any deep-rooted or difficult perennial weeds.

2 Add plenty of garden compost or rotted manure, then rake in a controlled-release fertilizer. Add these before laying a mulching sheet.

3 Cover the area with a weed-suppressing mulching sheet. You can use a plastic sheet, but a special woven mulching sheet is much better.

4 Make crossed slits through the sheet where you want to plant. Avoid making the slits too large.

5 Excavate planting holes and firm in the plants. If necessary tease a few of the roots apart first.

6 Water thoroughly, and keep well watered. Remove the sheet once the plants are well established.

GROUND COVER PLANTS

Some of the best plants for the job are *Armeria maritima*, bergenias, *Cotoneaster dammeri*, *Euonymus fortunei* varieties, *Hypericum calycinum*, and *Pachysandra terminalis*. If you want flowers as the main feature, heathers are a possibility.

HOW TO PLANT CREEPING GROUND COVER

The mulching sheet method is a good way to get clump-forming plants such as heathers off to a good start, but don't use it for those that creep and root, such as ajugas and *Hypericum calycinum*. Plant these normally but apply a loose mulch about 2in thick to cover the soil.

GRAVEL GARDENS

Gravel is an inexpensive and flexible alternative to paving or a lawn, although it is not suitable for a patio. It blends beautifully with plants, needs little maintenance, and can be used in both formal and informal designs. It is also a useful 'filler' material to use among other hard surfaces, or in irregularly shaped areas where paving will not easily fit and a lawn would be difficult to mow.

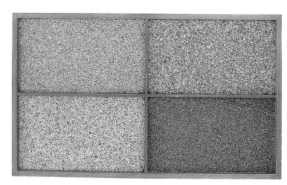

LEFT: *Gravels naturally vary considerably in color.*

Types of gravel

Gravel comes in many different shapes, sizes and colors. Some types are angular, others rounded, some are white, others assorted shades of green or red. All of them will look different in sun or shade, when wet or dry. The subtle change of color and mood is one of the appeals of gravel. The gravels available will depend on where you live, and which ones can be transported economically from further afield. Shop around first going to garden centers and builders merchants to see what is available in your area before making your choice.

Gravel paths

Gravel is often used for drives, but it is also a good choice for informal paths within the garden. It conforms to any shape so is useful for paths that meander. However, it is not a good choice for paths where you will have to wheel the mower.

HOW TO LAY A GRAVEL PATH

1 Excavate the area to a depth of approximately 6in, and ram the base firm.

2 Provide a stout edge to retain the gravel. For a straight path, battens secured by pegs about 3ft apart is an easy and inexpensive method.

3 First place a layer of compacted hardcore. Add a mixture of sand and coarse gravel (you can use sand and gravel mixture sold as ballast). Rake level and tamp or roll until firm.

4 Fill up to the required height with the final grade of gravel. In small gardens, the size often known as pea gravel looks good and is easy to walk on. Rake and roll repeatedly until the surface is firm and stable.

If the path is wide, it is a good idea to build the gravel up towards the center slightly so that puddles do not form after heavy rain.

Gravel beds

Gravel can be used as a straight substitute for grass and requires much less maintenance. You can even convert an existing lawn very simply by applying a weedkiller to the grass, laying edging blocks around the edge, then filling up with gravel.

Informal gravel beds still require some kind of edging restraint to prevent the gravel from spreading. If the bed is surrounded by a lawn, simply make sure that the graveled area is about 2in below the surrounding grass.

Other practical ways to prevent the gravel from scattering onto beds and other unwanted areas are to create a slightly sunken garden or to raise the surround slightly with a suitable edging.

Informal gravel areas often look especially effective if some plants are grown through the gravel – either in beds with seamless edges where the gravel goes over them, or as individual specimen plants.

HOW TO LAY A GRAVEL BED

1 Excavate the area to the required depth – about 2in of gravel is sufficient in most cases.

2 Level the ground. Lay heavy-duty black plastic or a mulching sheet over the area. Overlap the strips by approximately 2in.

3 Then tip the gravel on top and rake level.

4 To plant through the gravel, draw it back from the planting area and make a slit in the plastic sheet. Plant normally, enriching the soil beneath if necessary.

5 Firm in and pull back the plastic sheet before re-covering with gravel.

FORMING BOUNDARIES

Mᴏꜱᴛ ᴏꜰ ᴜꜱ ʜᴀᴠᴇ ᴀɴ ɪɴꜱᴛɪɴᴄᴛɪᴠᴇ ᴅᴇꜱɪʀᴇ ᴛᴏ mark our territory with a very visible boundary. It gives us a sense of privacy and the illusion of security, but above all it marks out our plot of land, the area in which we create our own very special paradise.

The problem with a small garden is that the boundary forms a large part of the garden, and the chances are that you will see it from whichever direction you look. In a large garden the boundary often merges into the background, but in a small one it can easily dominate.

Tall walls can be an asset – the walled town garden has many of the treasured attributes of an old walled country garden – but drab wooden fences and large overgrown hedges pose real problems if you want to make your garden look smart and stylish.

Don't take your boundary for granted, and never assume it can't be improved. Replacing a fence or pulling out a long-established hedge are not projects to be tackled lightly – they can be expensive or labor-intensive. Never make changes until you have consulted neighbors who

LEFT: *This is an excellent example of a combination boundary – a wooden picket fence supported on a low wall, with an escallonia flowering hedge growing through it.*

OPPOSITE ABOVE: *Walls make secure boundaries, but to prevent them looking oppressive cover with climbers, and if possible create a view beyond, as this attractive gate has done.*

OPPOSITE: *A wall as tall as this can easily dominate a small garden, but by treating it boldly and using it as a feature it becomes an asset.*

are affected. The boundary may belong to them, in which case it is not yours to change unilaterally. Even if it is legally yours to replace, the courtesy of discussing changes with others affected will go a long way to helping you remain on good terms with your neighbors.

Although you are unlikely to want to exceed them in a small garden, there may be legal limitations on boundary height, perhaps laid down in the terms of the contract when you bought the property. In some countries there may be restrictions placed by the highway department on road safety rights of way.

Restrictions are most likely in front gardens – some 'open plan' developments, for example, may have limitations on anything that might infringe the integrated structure of the gardens.

None of these restrictions need inhibit good garden design, but it is always worth checking whether any restrictions exist before erecting or planting a new boundary.

HEDGES FOR SMALL GARDENS

Many of the classic hedges, such as beech, yew, tall conifers (like × *Cupressocyparis leylandii*) and even the privet (*Ligustrum ovalifolium*) have strictly limited use in a small garden. In small gardens the emphasis should be on plants that have much to offer or compact growth. The hedges suggested here are just some of the plants that could be used to mark your boundary without being dull or oppressive. Be prepared to experiment with others.

Clipped formality

The classic box hedge (*Buxus sempervirens*) is still one of the best. It clips well and can be kept compact, but choose the variety 'Suffruticosa' if you want a really dwarf hedge like those seen in knot gardens. A quick-growing substitute is *Lonicera nitida*, and there's a golden form that always looks bright – but be prepared to cut frequently. Some of the dwarf barberries stand close clipping – try the red-leaved *Berberis thunbergii* 'Atropurpurea Nana'. Yew (*Taxus baccata*) is also excellent for formal clipping, and it can be kept compact enough for a small garden.

Colorful informal hedges

If you want to cut down on clipping, and want something brighter and more colorful than most foliage hedges, try the gray-leafed *Senecio* 'Sunshine' or the golden *Philadelphus coronarius* 'Aureus' (unfortunately sheds its leaves in winter). *Viburnum tinus* can also be kept to a reasonable height, and provided you avoid pruning out the new flowers it will bloom in winter. Many of the flowering and foliage barberries also make good 'shrubby' hedges. These will lack a neatly clipped profile, but pruning and shaping is normally only an annual job.

ABOVE: *Although* Lonicera nitida *needs frequent clipping, it makes a neat formal hedge.*

LEFT: *Many shrub roses can make an attractive flowering hedge in summer, but do not plant them too close to the edge of a path otherwise their thorny stems may be a nuisance.*

Using roses

Roses make delightful – and often fragrant – boundaries, but they have shortcomings. Their summer beauty is matched by winter ugliness, and they are not a good choice for a boundary where passers-by may be scratched by thorns. You can use a row of floribunda (cluster-flowered) roses, but the shrubby type are usually preferred for this job.

Old-fashioned lavender and rosemary dividers

Both these herbs make excellent informal flowering hedges, with the merit of being evergreen too. You could try the shorter lavender in front of the taller rosemary. Both become untidy with age, so replace the plants when it becomes necessary.

Other flowering hedges

Forsythia is one of the most popular flowering hedges, but careful pruning is required to achieve consistent flowering on a compact hedge. There are plenty of alternatives, including the shrubby potentillas, berberis like *B. × stenophylla*, with bold flowers, though this one can take up a lot of space, and even tall varieties of heathers if you just want a boundary marker rather than a barrier.

ABOVE: *Box is one of the classic plants to use for clipped formality. This is a glaucous form.*

HOW TO PLANT A NEW HEDGE

1 Prepare the ground very thoroughly. Excavate a trench – ideally about 2ft wide – and fork in plenty of rotten manure or garden compost.

2 Add a balanced fertilizer at the rate recommended by the manufacturer. Use a controlled-release fertilizer if planting in the autumn.

3 Use a garden line, stretched along the center of the trench, as a positioning guide. If the area is windy or you need a particularly dense hedge, plant a double row of trees. Bare-root plants are cheaper than container-grown plants, but only separate them and expose the roots once you are ready to plant. Only the most popular hedging plants are likely to be available bare-root, and for many of the plants suggested you will have to plant a single row of container-grown plants.

4 Use a piece of wood or a cane cut to the appropriate length as a guide for even spacing. Make sure the roots are well spread out. If planting container-grown plants, tease out some of the roots that are running around the edge of the root-ball.

5 Firm the plants in well and water thoroughly. Be prepared to water the hedge regularly in dry weather for the first season. Keep down weeds until the hedge is well established, then it should suppress the weeds naturally.

GARDEN WALLS

Except for special cases, such as basement flats and the need for privacy or screening in a difficult neighborhood, high walls are inappropriate for a small garden. However, low walls up to about 3–4ft in height are a useful alternative to a hedge, particularly if you want to avoid regular trimming. Although the rain shadow and shade problems remain the same whether you have a wall or a hedge, a wall will not impoverish the soil in the same way as a hedge.

Low walls

A low wall, say 1–2ft tall, will serve the same demarcation function as a taller one, but in more appropriate scale for a small garden, and shrubs planted behind it are more likely to thrive. Modest garden walls like this are much easier to construct than tall ones, which may need substantial reinforcing piers, and are well within the scope of a competent garden handyman to build.

Brick walls

Plain brick walls can harmonize with the house, but generally look dull from a design viewpoint. A skilled bricklayer can often add interest by laying panels or strips in a different pattern. The choice of brick and the capping will also alter the appearance. Some are capped with bricks, others have special coping tiles. These all add to the subtle variety of brick walls.

Block walls

Many manufacturers of concrete paving slabs also produce walling blocks made from the same material. These are especially useful for internal garden walls and raised beds. They are often colored to resemble natural stone, but brighter colors are available if you want to match the color scheme used for the paving. Bear in mind that colors will weather and become much more muted within a couple of years.

ABOVE: *Brick walls needn't be boring.*
RIGHT: *A wall like this makes a solid and secure boundary without making the garden appear too enclosed.*

Screen block walls

Screen block walls (sometimes called pierced block) are most frequently used for internal walls, perhaps around the patio or to divide one part of the garden from another, but they can also be used to create a striking boundary wall too.

These blocks have to be used with special piers and topped with the appropriate coping. They are useful if you want to create a modern image, or perhaps the atmosphere of a Mediterranean garden.

Mixing materials

Some of the smartest boundary walls are made from more than one material. Screen blocks look good as panels within a concrete walling block framework. Screen blocks can also be incorporated into a brick wall, and help to let light through and to filter some of the wind. Panels of flint or other stone can be set into an otherwise boring tall brick wall.

BELOW: *Walls can be colorful . . . if you create planting areas. The summer bedding plants used here are replaced at the end of the season with bulbs and spring bedding plants to use the planting areas to their full advantage.*

Cavity walls

Low cavity walls that can be lined with plants soon become an eye-catching feature. Pack them with colorful summer flowers, or plant with permanent perennials such as dwarf conifers, which maintain interest throughout the year (but be sure to choose true dwarf conifers for this). If you plant cascading forms

ABOVE: *Dry stone walls are not difficult to build provided you keep them low, and you can plant into the sides for extra interest.*

such as nasturtium or trailing lobelia, the effect can be really stunning. For a spring display, try aubrieta and the yellow *Aurinia saxatilis*, with a few dwarf spring-flowering bulbs.

Dry stone walling

Dry stone walls are more often used for retaining banks or as internal dividers, but in an appropriate setting this kind of wall makes an attractive boundary. This type of wall looks best where dry stone walls are part of the natural landscape.

The great advantage of a dry stone wall – which is assembled without mortar – is the ability to plant in the sides. This can provide a home for many kinds of rock plants.

Walls with a difference

The larger and taller the wall, the more imaginative you should be when designing it. Try incorporating an alcove for an ornament, or a panel into which you can set an artistic piece of wrought-iron that can be viewed against the green of a neighboring field or garden.

WALL BUILDING MATERIALS

Most builders' merchants stock a good range of bricks; the majority are suitable for garden walls, but if you need a lot – enough to justify ordering direct – get in touch with a few brick companies. Their expertise can be invaluable, and most will be able to offer you a wide choice.

Buying bricks is something most of us do only rarely, so professional advice is especially useful. The author's experience, however, suggests that you can't always depend on the advice of a builder's merchant. Shop around until you find someone who really appears to have a knowledgeable passion for bricks – they will tell you about all the different finishes and colors available, and most importantly will know whether a particular brick is suitable for the job you have in mind. *Always* explain what you want your bricks for: a building, a garden wall, wall of a raised bed, or for paving. Some bricks which are perfectly suitable for house walls may be very unsuitable for paths or garden walls.

If you need a lot of bricks (many hundreds), it may be better, and cheaper, to buy direct from a brick manufacturer if they will deal with the general public.

ABOVE: *Bricks come in many colors and finishes, and these are just a small selection from the many kinds available. Names of* *bricks vary from country to country, but whatever names are used you are likely to have a good choice.*

MASONRY MORTAR

A suitable mortar for brick-laying can be made from 1 part cement to 3 parts soft sand. Parts are by volume and not weight. Cement dyes can be added to create special effects, but use colored mortar with care.

Common bonds

Expert brick-layers may use more complicated bonds, but for ordinary garden walls – and especially those that you are likely to lay yourself, perhaps for a low boundary wall or for a raised bed within the garden – it is best to choose one of the three bonds illustrated below.

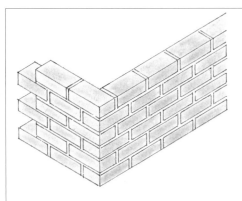

Running bond or stretcher bond This is the simplest form of bonding, and is used for walls a single brick wide – or where you want to create a cavity, such as a low wall with a planting space.

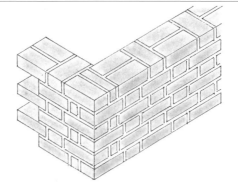

Flemish bond This is another way to create a strong bond in a wall two bricks wide. The bricks are laid both lengthways and across the wall within the same course.

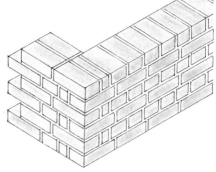

English bond This is used for a thick wall the width of two bricks laid side by side – useful where strength is needed for a high wall. Alternate courses are laid lengthways then across the wall.

HOW TO LAY BRICKS AND BLOCKS

Although bricks are being laid here, the same principles apply to laying walling blocks.

1 All walls require a footing. The one shown here is a for a low wall just one brick wide: for larger and thicker walls the dimensions of the footing will have to be increased.

Excavate a trench about 12in deep, and place about 5in of consolidated hardcore in the bottom. Drive pegs in so that the tops are at the final height of the base. Use a spirit-level to check levels.

2 Fill with a concrete mix of 1 part cement, 2½ parts sharp sand and 3½ parts ¾in aggregate, and level it off with the peg tops.

3 When the concrete has hardened for a few days, lay the bricks on a bed of mortar, also place a wedge of mortar at one end of each brick to be laid. For stability, always make a pier at each end, and at intervals of about 6–8ft if the wall is long. Here two bricks have been laid cross-ways for this purpose.

4 For subsequent courses, lay a ribbon of mortar on top of the previous row, then 'butter' one end of the brick to be laid.

5 Tap level, checking constantly with a spirit-level.

6 The wall must be finished off with a coping of suitable bricks or with special coping sold for the purpose.

BOUNDARY FENCES

Fences have the great merit of being more instant than hedges and less expensive than walls. That is the reason they are so often chosen by builders for new properties, and why they are frequently chosen again when the original fences come to the end of their useful life.

Closeboard and panel fences are popular, but predictable and a little boring. There are plenty of styles to choose from, however, so select a fence appropriate to your garden design yet practical for the purposes you have in mind.

If you want privacy or animal-proofing, you will have to opt for one of the solid styles, but if it is just a boundary-marker that is needed there are many attractive fences that look stylish and won't appear oppressive in a small garden.

The names of particular fence types may vary from country to country. If you do not recognize any of the names here check with the pictures.

Closeboard

Closeboard fencing is erected on site by nailing overlapping feather-edged boards to horizontal rails already secured to stout upright posts. It is a strong, secure fence, but not particularly attractive – especially viewed from the side with the rails.

Panels

Prefabricated panels are quick and easy to erect and therefore a popular choice. Panels are usually about 6ft long and range in height from about 2ft to 6ft, generally in 1ft steps. The interwoven or overlapping boards are sandwiched between a frame of sawn lumber. The woven style is not as peep-proof as overlapping boards.

Interlap or hit-and-miss

This combines strength and a solid appearance with better wind-filtering than a solid fence (which can create turbulent eddies that may be damaging to plants). It is constructed from

ABOVE: *Closeboard fencing well covered with climbing roses.*

ABOVE: *Wattle or woven fences make an attractive background for plants.*

ABOVE: *A low wooden fence is not obtrusive and can look very attractive.*

square-edged boards that are nailed to the horizontal rails on alternate sides. Overlapping the edges gives more privacy, while spacing them further apart can look more decorative.

Picket

Picket fences look good in country gardens, but can also be a smart choice for a small town garden. Narrow, vertical pales are nailed to horizontal timbers, spaced about 5cm (2in) apart. You can make them yourself or buy kits with some of the laborious work done for you. The simplest shape for the top of each pale is a point, but you can make them rounded or choose a more ornate finial shape. A picket fence can be left in natural wood color, but they look particularly smart painted white. Because they are usually relatively low, and you can see plenty of garden through the well-spaced pales, they don't dominate the garden in the same way as a tall, solid fence.

Ranch-style

Ranch-style fences consist of broad horizontal rails fixed to stout upright posts. They are usually quite low, and frequently consist of just two or three rails. White-painted wood is a popular material, but wipe-down plastic equivalents are very convincing and easy to maintain. For a small garden they provide a clear boundary without becoming a visual obstruction. Also, rain and sun shadows are not created in the way that occurs with more solid fences.

Post and chain

This is the least obtrusive of all fences. Purely a boundary marker, it will do nothing to deter animals or children, or keep balls out of the garden, but it is a good choice if you want a fence that is hardly noticeable. You can use wooden, concrete or plastic posts and metal or plastic chains. Choose a white plastic chain if you want to make a feature of the fence, black if you want the chain to recede and blend into the background.

Chain link

Chain link is not an aesthetic choice, but it is highly practical and an effective barrier for animals. It is probably best to have a contractor erect a chain link fence, as it needs to be tensioned properly. You may like the fact that you can see through it, especially if the view beyond is attractive, but you may prefer to plant climbers beside it to provide a better screen. Choose tough evergreens such as ivy if you want year-round screening.

Bamboo

Bamboo is a natural choice if you've created an oriental-style garden, but don't be afraid to use this type of fence for any garden style if it looks right. Bamboo fences come in many shapes and sizes, and the one you adopt will depend partly on the availability and cost of the material and partly on your creativity and skill in building this kind of fence.

ABOVE: *A fence like this just needs a supply of bamboo and skill at tying knots!*

LEFT: *A white picket fence can make the boundary a feature of the garden.*

HOW TO ERECT A FENCE

Many gardeners prefer to employ a contractor to erect or replace a fence. They will certainly make lighter work of it with their professional tools for excavating post holes, and a speed that comes with expertise, but some fences are very easy to erect yourself. Two of the easiest are panel and ranch-type fences, which are illustrated in simple steps below.

HOW TO ERECT A PANEL FANCE

1 Post spikes are an easier option than excavating holes and concreting the post in position. The cost saving on using a shorter post and no concrete will go some way towards the cost of the spike.

Use a special tool to protect the spike top, then drive it in with a sledge-hammer. Check periodically with a spirit-level to ensure it is absolutely vertical.

2 Once the spike has been driven in, insert the post and check the vertical again.

3 Lay the panel in position on the ground and mark the position of the next post. Drive in the next spike, testing for the vertical again.

4 There are various ways to fix the panels to the posts, but panel brackets are easy to use.

5 Insert the panel and nail in position, through the brackets. Insert the post at the other end and nail the panel in position at that end.

6 Check the horizontal level both before and after nailing, and make any necessary adjustments before moving on to the next panel.

7 Finish off by nailing a post cap to the top of each post. This will keep water out of the end grain of the timber and extend its life.

HOW TO ERECT A RANCH-STYLE FENCE

1 Although ranch-style fences are easy to erect the posts must be well secured in the ground. For a wooden fence, use 5 × 4in posts, set at about 6½ft intervals. For additional strength add intermediate posts. A size of 3½in square is adequate for these.

Make sure the posts go at least 18in into the ground.

2 Concrete the posts into position, then screw or nail the planks in position, making sure fixings are rust-proof. Use a carpenter's level to make sure the planks are horizontal. Butt-join the planks in the center of a post, but try to stagger the joints on each row so that there is not a weak point in the fence.

3 Fit a post cap. This improves the appearance and also protects the posts. Paint with a good quality paint recommended for outdoor use.

ABOVE LEFT: *Panel fences are easily erected and provide a peep-proof barrier, but are best clothed with plants to soften the effect.*
ABOVE: *Ranch-style fences make an unobtrusive barrier – ideal where the garden merges into the countryside.*

THE PLASTIC ALTERNATIVE

There are many plastic ranch-style fences. They will vary slightly in the way they are assembled. Detailed instructions should come with them, however, and you should have no difficulty.

The 'planks' are sometimes available in different widths – 4in and 6in for example – and these help to create different visual appearances. Gates made from the same material are also available from some manufacturers.

Posts are usually concreted into the ground, and the cellular plastic planks are push-fitted into slots or special fittings. Special union pieces are used to join lengths, and post caps are usually glued and pushed into position.

White ranch fencing needs to be kept clean to look good, and plastic can simply be washed when it looks grubby.

SEE-THROUGH BOUNDARIES

The best boundary of all might be no boundary . . . at least none that you can see. The ha-ha, once popular with the great landscape gardeners of the past, was a successful way of achieving this. The boundary is a deep, wide ditch that can't easily be seen from within the garden, so the garden appears to continue into the rolling countryside beyond.

The ha-ha is not a technique easily adapted to a small modern garden, and totally inappropriate if you overlook a townscape instead of pleasant green fields. However, the principle of being able to blur the margin between your garden and your neighbor's garden, or perhaps open countryside if you are fortunate enough to have the option, is one worth pursuing.

Ditches

A ditch sounds an unattractive feature. However, if one happens to run along one of your boundaries it might be possible to make a feature of it, rather than trying to hide it. Try planting it with bog plants, and landscape it into your garden, perhaps with a pond and an extended bog garden linking the two.

Some people even try to create a ditch, using a liner that restricts water loss and flooding it with water periodically. Provided the view of the garden beyond is attractive, this is a sure-fire way to give your small garden an open style only normally associated with larger gardens.

Shared gardens

Like-minded gardening enthusiasts sometimes design their gardens so that they appear to be linked. Usually this is done by taking the lawn through a gap in the boundary and using shrubs or mixed borders that start in one garden and end in the next. This can work surprisingly well, and although each is responsible for his own area the illusion is that the garden goes on beyond.

If this seems too 'communal', the same effect can be achieved by making lawns and borders meet yet still retain an unobtrusive fence, such as a widely spaced post and rail fence, or even a few simple strands of wire – which can be almost invisible from a distance.

Alternatively, consider linking gardens with an attractive gate. You don't have to use it, but it will look as though there is more garden beyond to be explored.

Shrubby solutions

Although a continuous lawn can be employed to link adjoining gardens and make them look larger, you can instead agree to abolish the fence and both plant shrubs in a bed along the boundary. Even if a relatively narrow strip is used in each garden, the

ABOVE: *A window in the wall can immediately transform a potentially boring area of brick into a real focus point.*

impression will be of a much larger and more substantial shrub border with no sign of obtrusive fences.

Claire-voyée

The term means literally 'clear view', and came into use after the lawless Middle Ages in Europe when it became less necessary to enclose one's property with a solid wall, and apertures were cut in walls to allow the countryside beyond to be viewed from within.

If you have a view that is worth framing, you can introduce a claire-voyée 'window' in the wall of even a tiny garden.

BRIGHTENING UP FENCES AND WALLS

If replacing an existing old fence or wall simply isn't practical because of the time and expense involved, consider ways to camouflage or brighten up the old one.

Climbers

Climbers present one of the most pleasing ways to cover an unsightly wall or fence, but always make sure the fence is firm in its foundations first, otherwise the extra weight and wind resistance will just bring it down sooner and you will have to untangle the climber and repair the fence anyway.

For year-round cover, tough evergreens such as ivies are justifiably popular. They can be slow to establish, but ultimately provide dense cover and can easily be clipped back once or twice a year to prevent the shoots encroaching beyond their territory.

For summer-only cover, try the vigorous hop (*Humulus lupulus*), especially in its very attractive golden form 'Aureus'. Once established, one plant will cover a large area of fence.

For flowers, some of the clematis can be very successful, though winter is an unattractive time. Tall-growing species such as *Clematis montana* sound unlikely candidates, but they will run along the fence and cascade down each side instead of climbing, and the pink *C. m. rubens* looks particularly splendid.

Trained trees

Trained fruit trees can transform a tall wall or fence and turn it into a real feature when laden with flowers or fruit. Even in winter the bare stems of a fan or espalier tree can look dramatic, especially if picked out against a white-painted wall.

Training from scratch is difficult and time-consuming, and it is worth buying ready-trained trees.

RIGHT: *Old fences discolor and look drab and shabby with age. This is one way to transform a dull fence.*

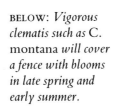

BELOW: *Vigorous clematis such as* C. montana *will cover a fence with blooms in late spring and early summer.*

A coat of paint

A drab old wall can be transformed with a coat of masonry paint. White reflects the light well, but any pale color can look pleasing, particularly when contrasted with greenery.

Grow striking plants like phormiums or yuccas in front so that their strong profiles are picked out against the background, or stand groups of containers so that they are backed by the painted wall.

Framed effects

Fences are more difficult to paint as a backdrop for plants, and you must be careful about paint seeping through to your neighbor's side, but a little localized painting could work well.

Try a large white circle within which you can frame a striking plant as a focal point. Instead of painting the actual fence, try cutting out a large wooden circle and painting that – then pin it to the fence.

FINISHING TOUCHES

A SMALL GARDEN SHOULD BE FULL OF SURPRISES, packed with finishing touches that compensate for the lack of scope offered by limited size.

Many of the focal point techniques used in large gardens can be scaled down and applied on a small scale, and even in a small space the garden can express the owner's sense of fun and personality in the little extras that are grafted onto the basic design.

The whole area can be made to work, every corner can be exploited with devices if not plants, and a degree of flexibility can be built in that makes variety a real possibility.

ABOVE: *A seat like this suggests a gardener with a strong sense of design.*

OPPOSITE ABOVE: *Ornaments have been used to excellent effect here. A sundial commands center stage and the eye is taken across the garden to a figure which adds light and life.*

OPPOSITE BELOW: *Figures usually look best framed by plants.*

LEFT: *This quiet corner has been transformed by white-painted trellis and seat.*

In a large garden most ornaments, furniture and fixtures like garden lights are a static part of the design. In a small garden a slight rearrangement of the furniture, the changed position of a light, or the simple exchange of one ornament for another according to mood and season means that the garden need never be predictable despite limitations of size.

Ornaments in particular can set a tone for the garden: serious or frivolous, classic or modern. They suggest the owner's taste . . . and even sense of humor. Just as the painting on the living-room wall or the ornaments on the sideboard can tell you a lot about the occupier, so garden ornaments reveal the personality of the garden maker.

Garden lighting can be practical and even a useful security measure, but it also offers scope for artistic interpretation. Experiment with spotlights in various positions and discover the dramatically different effects created by the use of light and shadows from different angles.

Arches and pergolas are a more permanent element of the garden's design, but they don't have to be planned in at the design stage and are easily added to an existing garden.

PERGOLAS AND ARCHES

A sense of height is important even in a small garden. Unless there is vertical use of plants or upright garden features, the center of the garden will be flat. Attention will pass over the center and go instead to the edges of the garden: exactly the lifeless effect you want to avoid.

Small trees, wall shrubs and climbers can provide the necessary verticals, but if these are in short supply an arch or pergola may be the answer.

Traditionally, and especially in cottage gardens, they have been made from rustic poles, but where they adjoin the house or link home with patio, sawn lumber is a better choice. The various constructions described here are free-standing, and usually used as plant supports. Their visual effect is to take the eye to further down the garden.

If a pergola or arch seems inappropriate, similar construction techniques can be used to create an intimate arbor.

HOW TO ASSEMBLE AN ARCH

The simplest way to make an arch is to use a kit, which only needs assembling.

1 First establish the post positions, allowing 1ft between the edge of the path and post, so that plants do not obstruct the path.

2 Fence spikes are the easiest way to fix the posts. Drive them in using a protective dolly. Check frequently with a carpenter's level. Insert the posts and tighten the spikes around them. Alternatively, excavate four holes, each to the depth of 2ft.

3 Position the legs of the arch in the holes. Fill in with the excavated earth, and compact.

4 Lay the halves of the overhead beams on a flat surface, and carefully screw the joint together with rust-proof screws.

5 Fit the overhead beams to the posts – in this example they slot into the tops of the posts and are nailed in place.

HOW TO JOIN RUSTIC POLES

Rustic arches and pergolas look particularly attractive covered with roses or other climbers. You can be creative with the designs, but the same few basic joints shown here are all that you will need.

1 To fix horizontal poles to vertical ones, saw a notch of a suitable size for the horizontal piece to fit snugly.

2 If you have to join two horizontal pieces, saw two opposing and matching notches so that one sits over the other, and secure them.

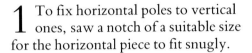

3 To fix cross-pieces to horizontals or uprights, remove a V-shaped notch using a chisel if necessary to achieve a snug fit, then nail into place with rust-proof nails.

4 Use halving joints where two pieces cross. Make two saw cuts half way through the pole, then remove the waste timber with a chisel.

5 Secure the joint with a nail. For extra strength, paint the joint with woodworking adhesive first.

6 Bird's mouth joints are useful for connecting horizontal or diagonal pieces to uprights. Cut out a V-shaped notch about 1in deep, and saw the other piece to match. Use a chisel to achieve a good fit.

7 Try out the assembly on the ground, then insert the uprights in prepared holes and make sure these are secure before adding any horizontal or top pieces. Most pieces can be nailed together, but screw any sections subject to stress.

ABOVE: *Rustic poles are an appropriate choice for a feature like this.*

USING ORNAMENTS

Ornaments can be used around the garden in much the same way as around the house. Choose them simply because you like them, because they will look good in a particular position, or as a device for attracting attention and admiration.

In a small garden their use as a focal point is paramount. Large focal points are impractical or can only ever be few in number, but small ornaments, birdbaths, sundials, and attractive urns can be used liberally. The only 'rule' is not to have more than a couple in view at once, as they will then compete for attention rather than taking center stage. There is no limit to the number you can use in a small garden provided they form part of a journey of discovery. Use them among plants that you discover only from a particular viewpoint, or around a corner that is not visible from where you viewed the previous focal point.

Never let ornaments detract from major focal points that form part of the basic design, and don't allow the garden to look cluttered. Aim for simplicity with surprises.

RIGHT: *A bird bath is a better choice than a sundial for a position often in shade.*

BELOW: *A chimney pot makes an unusual plinth for a sundial.*

Sundials

Whole books are written about sundials, and purists expect them to be functional. Setting them up accurately not only demands a sunny spot but quite a lot of calculations too, with compensation for geographical position. Most of us, using the sundial simply as an ornament, are happy to go out at noon on a sunny day in summer and align the gnomon to give the appropriate reading. It won't be accurate as the seasons change, but then you are unlikely to be using it to decide when it is time to leave for the office.

Accuracy may not be important, but a sunny position is. The whole object of a sundial is lost in a shady

spot, where a birdbath would serve a similar design function without looking incongruous.

Choose the plinth carefully – they vary in style and height (you could even build your own from bricks) and go for a fairly low plinth if the area available is quite small.

The best place for a sundial is as a centerpiece for a formal garden, perhaps in the center of a herb garden with paths radiating out from the center. The lawn is another practical choice, but if the lawn is small, consider placing the sundial to one side rather than in the center.

Birdbaths

The positions suggested for a sundial are also appropriate for a birdbath, but birdbaths are much more useful for shady positions – though not too close to trees, otherwise they become filled with leaves and debris. A birdbath can even look effective in a flower border, with much of the plinth covered by flowers, or try it as a patio ornament if you want the pleasures of watching the birds drinking from it and bathing.

Sculptures

The use of sculptures and artistic objects demands confidence. Few people react aversely to a sundial or birdbath, but sculptures or artistic ornaments that generate admiration in one person can be abhorrent to another. This should never deter anyone from using ornaments that please them, but they are bound to be somewhat more difficult to place in a small garden.

Human figures

Busts sound unlikely ornaments for a small garden, but provided they aren't too large they can look great in an alcove or on a plinth in a dull corner. Small figures can sometimes work well if surrounded by clever planting.

Animal figures

Animal figures are always a safe bet, especially if set among the plants, or even on the lawn.

Abstract ornaments

Abstract ornaments should be used with restraint – they make a considerable impact. Too many will tend to make the area look more like an art gallery than a garden.

Wall masks, plaques and gargoyles

These are great for relieving a dull wall, but are almost always best set amid the leaves of a climber such as ivy. The foliage frames the feature, and emphasizes its role as an unusual focal point.

Gnomes

You probably love them or hate them, and that is the problem with using gnomes. One or two little people cleverly used with restraint can be very effective and add a sense of fun, but usually either they are banished from the garden or there is a whole army of them. It may be with the latter approach that the garden will simply appear as a setting for a gnome collection.

Plinths and pedestals

Plinths are essential for raising a sundial, birdbath or bust to an appropriate height, but they can look stark in a small garden. Make more of a feature of a plinth by planting some low-growing plants around the base, and then use a few tall ground cover plants that can gradually stretch up around the base.

A plinth can look severe on a lawn and mowing around it can be tedious. Try setting one in a gravel bed with alpines around the base, or leave the bed as soil and plant thyme or other low-growing aromatic herbs.

ABOVE: *Small animal figures creeping out from the plants add a sense of fun.*

ABOVE: *This kind of ornament needs careful placing in a small garden – always take time to consider position.*

RIGHT: *Figures are often more exciting when they are discovered among the plants.*

GARDEN LIGHTING

Garden lights not only make your garden look more dramatic as dusk falls, they also extend the hours during which you can enjoy it. If you like entertaining in the garden on summer evenings, or just want to sit and relax, lights will add another dimension to the space.

When illuminating your garden you are not attempting to fill the garden with floodlights, but rather to use spotlights to pick out a particular tree, highlight an ornament, or bring to life the droplets of a cascade or fountain.

You don't even need elaborate electric lines. Low-voltage lighting supplied from a transformer indoors is perfectly adequate for most lighting jobs in a small garden.

Lighting beds
Summer bedding looks good with pools of light thrown downwards onto the beds. If you find the units obtrusive during the day, choose a low-voltage type that is easy to move around. Simply push the spiked supports into the bed when you want to use the garden in the evening.

Picking out plants
Use a spotlight to pick out one or two striking plants that will form focal points in the evening. The white bark of a birch tree, perhaps underplanted with white impatiens, the tall ramrod spikes of red hot pokers (kniphofias), or a spiky yucca, make excellent focal points picked out in a spotlight. Tall feathery plants, such as fennel, also illuminate well.

Spotlighting ornaments
Ornaments and containers full of plants also make striking features to pick out in a spotlight.

Before highlighting an ornament, try moving the beam around. Quite different effects can be achieved by directing it upwards or downwards, and side lighting creates a very different effect to straight-on illumination.

ABOVE: *An illuminated garden can become magical as dusk falls, and you will derive many more hours of pleasure from being able to sit out in the evening.*

Illuminating water
Underwater lighting is popular and you can buy special sealed lamps designed to be submerged or to float, but the effect can be disappointing if the water is murky or if algae grows thickly on the lenses. A simple white spotlight playing on moving water is often the most effective.

THINKING OF THE NEIGHBORS

There is a problem with using garden lights in a small garden: you have to consider neighbors. It is unsociable to fix a spotlight where the beam not only illuminates your favorite tree but also falls on the windows of your neighbor's house. If you direct beams downwards rather than upwards, the pools of light should not intrude.

LEFT: *The best garden lighting is not obtrusive or unattractive during the day, and throws off white light when illuminated.*

HOW TO INSTALL LOW-VOLTAGE LIGHTING

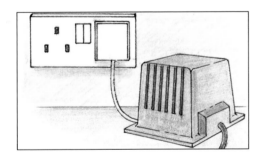

2 Drill a hole through the window frame or wall, just wide enough to take the cable. Fill in any gaps afterwards, using a mastic or other waterproof filler.

1 A low-voltage lighting kit will come with a transformer. This must always be positioned in a dry place indoors or in a garage or outbuilding.

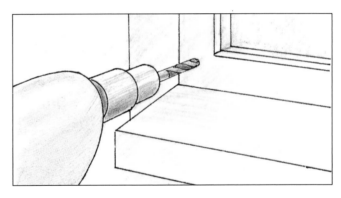

3 Although the cable carries a low voltage and you will not be electrocuted, it is still a potential hazard if left lying on the surface where someone might trip over it. Unless the lights are to be positioned close to where the cable emerges from indoors, run it underground in a conduit.

4 Most low-voltage lighting systems are designed so that the lamps are easy to position and to move around. Many of them can just be pushed into the ground wherever you choose to place them.

FURNISHING THE GARDEN

A few seats and a table make the garden an inviting place to eat, or to sit and relax. Unfortunately where space is at a premium every item has to be chosen and placed with care. Built-in seats, and especially tree seats, are a good choice for a small garden.

Portable furniture

Furniture that can be moved is useful for a quick scene change and helps to prevent your garden becoming predictable. It is surprising how effective a canvas 'director's chair' can look on a summer's day, and it is quick and easy to fold up and store when not in use.

Built-in

Built-in furniture saves space and helps prevent a small garden looking cluttered. The best place for built-in seating is the patio, where it can often be designed along with the rest of the structure. White-painted planks look smart, and can quickly be transformed with cushions to look elegant as well as feel comfortable.

Built-round

A tree seat makes an eye-catching garden feature, and this is one occasion when the advice not to have a seat beneath a tree can be ignored! White paint will help the seat to stand out in the shade of its branches.

Wrought and cast iron

Genuine cast and wrought iron furniture is expensive and very heavy, but alloy imitations are available with all the charm of the original but at a more manageable price and weight. White is again a popular color, but bear in mind that although this type of furniture can stand outside throughout the year, it will soon become dirty – and cleaning the intricate patterns isn't easy. Green looks just as smart yet doesn't show the dirt.

Use cushions to add patches of color, and to make the chairs more comfortable to sit on!

LEFT: White-painted metal furniture looks tasteful and can help enliven a dull corner of the garden.

BELOW: A charming wooden seat.

BELOW LEFT: A reconstituted stone seat has a timeless appeal that beckons you to sit and rest.

Wooden seats and benches

Wooden seats can be left in natural wood color to blend with the background or painted so that they become a focal point. White is popular, but green and even red can look very smart. Marine paint is weather-resistant.

Plastic

Don't dismiss plastic. Certainly there are plenty of unattractive pieces of garden furniture made from this material, but the better pieces can look very stylish for a patio in the setting of a modern garden.

HOW TO MAKE A TREE SEAT

1 Start by securing the legs in position. Use 1½ × 3in soft wood such as pine, treated with a preservative. You will need eight lengths about 27in long. Concrete them into position.

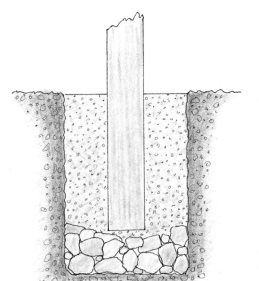

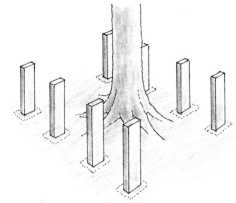

2 Position the legs about 15–18in apart in two rows about the same distance either side of the trunk.

3 Cut four pieces of 1 × 2in soft wood for the cross-bars. Allow 3in overhang at each end.

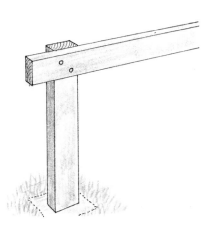

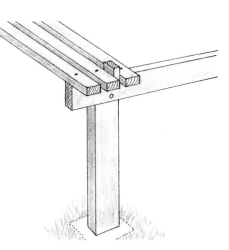

4 Drill and screw these to the posts. Then, cut slats to the required length (the number will depend on the size of your seat). Allow for a 1in space between each slat. Paint the slats and cross-bars with white paint (or a wood preservative or stain if you prefer), and allow to dry before final assembly. Test the spacing, using an offcut of wood as a guide, and when satisfied that they are evenly spaced on the cross-bars, mark the positions with a pencil. Then glue and nail into position.

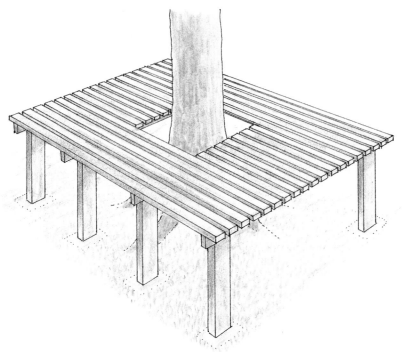

CONTAINER CHOICES

MANY PLANT CONTAINERS ARE PURELY
practical: plain clay pots, unadorned plastic
windowboxes or wooden troughs that are
functional but not inspiring. There is nothing
wrong with any of these if they are to be covered
with trailers and cascading blooms, but most
plants have an upright habit and an interesting
container forms part of the display and becomes
an important feature.

Containers are especially useful in a small
garden because they bring life and color, or just
subtle shades of green, to corners that might
otherwise remain bare. By hanging interesting or
colorful containers on bleak walls, by using them
alongside the steps to a basement garden, or
simply using tubs by the front door, containers
make the most of all the available space.

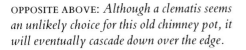

LEFT: Don't discard the old metal watering-can. It can be painted and pressed into use for plants such as ivies.

FAR LEFT: This old copper boiler has found new life as a container for tulips and pansies.

OPPOSITE ABOVE: Although a clematis seems an unlikely choice for this old chimney pot, it will eventually cascade down over the edge.

OPPOSITE BELOW: Containers are invaluable in a small garden as they can be used to take advantage of any spare space.

BELOW: It is surprising how much you can do with a roof garden, by growing a wide range of plants in containers.

Don't confine your choice of container plants to summer bedding and spring bulbs, however. If you do, your containers will look like monuments to past glories for many months of the year. Plant evergreen shrubs, or groups of evergreen border plants. Use short-term pot plants in the winter and don't be afraid to discard them after a few weeks.

Houseplants can be used in summer to add a touch of the exotic to your patio. Provided they are carefully acclimatized first (placed in a sheltered position, and protected from winds and strong sun, perhaps with a covering of horticultural fleece for the first week), you can use them to create tropical corners. It's best to use only those plants with thick or fleshy leaves.

Be bold. Use kitchen utensils such as pots and pans as containers, old chimney pots, drainpipes, boots and shoes, but always make sure that there are drainage holes.

You can even make large clay pots more interesting by painting on an attractive design with masonry paint. Use a stencil if you are not artistically inclined.

POTS FOR DOORWAY DECORATION

Always choose an imposing plant in an attractive container to go by the front door, and if possible one that looks good for a long period.

This is the place for a clipped bay in an ornate pot or Versailles tub, or an attractive bamboo in an oriental-style container.

If you have chosen imposing plants to go by the front door supplement these with a group of smaller containers that add seasonal color, and perhaps scent. Don't be afraid to move pots around to maintain interest. Keep a small lilac in a tub or grow pots of hyacinths and move them to the front door as they come into flower to add a heady perfume.

Formal shrubs

If space really is limited and the rest of the garden has a formal style, a couple of clipped or trained evergreens can look elegant throughout the year. Clipped bays are good, but in cold areas are likely to suffer from damaged leaves in winter, but many conifers have a naturally formal outline and remain attractive throughout the year with minimal attention. Box can be bought clipped into topiary shapes, and though expensive to buy will add instant impact. You can easily buy a box plant and clip it into a ball or pyramid

LEFT: *Remember to appeal to the sense of smell as well as sight. Here lavender not only co-ordinates, but it adds a touch of fragrance as well.*

BELOW LEFT: *Formally clipped box can be expensive to buy, but with patience you can train your own. They are ideal for a formal setting.*

BELOW: *Don't forget that pots can always be used to grow well-trained shrubs.*

shape over the course of a couple of years, if you are happy with a simple geometric shape.

Scented delights

Scent always arouses comment from visitors to the door. In winter you will have to rely on bulbs like hyacinths and *Iris danfordiae*. In spring follow these with daphne and then lilac (both indifferent for the rest of the year, so be prepared to move them to a less conspicuous part of the garden after flowering).

Summer brings the opportunity to use scented bedding plants such as flowering tobacco plants and stocks.

Climbers in pots

A climber around the door always looks attractive, and you can usually erect a trellis for support. If there is a choice, plant directly into the ground, but if that is not possible, pot a climber in a tub. Large-flowered clematis will do well, and even a honeysuckle. You can try a climbing or rambling rose, but these are more demanding in pots.

GROUPING POTS AND PLANTS

If isolated pots seem to lack impact, try grouping them together – the mutual support they lend each other gives them a strength that they lack individually. If the pots are rather plain, placing smaller ones in front will mask those behind and bring the display almost to ground level.

Groups in the porch

Make a bold display in a porch by using tall plants, especially evergreen shrubs, at the back and smaller flowering plants in front.

If space is limited, instead of going for a lush effect with lots of foliage and flowers, concentrate on the containers rather than the plants. Decorative pots are often available as matching sets. Grouping these together looks good even if the plants they contain are only mediocre.

Groups in corners

Difficult corners are an ideal place in which to use containers to create color, filling in a spare piece of ground where nothing much seems to do well. Patios usually have corners that would otherwise remain unused. Group shrubs or tall houseplants at the back and colorful summer bedding plants in front, along with bright-leaved indoor plants for the warmest months.

Alternatively, choose a small group of elegant containers and use the plants in a more restrained way. A trailer growing from a pedestal container with a cluster of distinctive small pots around the base can be as eye-catching as a large group.

In a dull corner, perhaps formed where two wooden fences join, or where house joins fence in a sunless position, try making a bed of small-sized gravel on which to place a group of terracotta pots. Red gravel will help to bring color. Fill the pots with bright annuals for the summer, and winter-flowering pansies and bulbs for winter and spring. Try spacing the pots out and adding a few interesting pieces of rock among them.

ABOVE LEFT: *Grouping plants in a porch makes a high-impact feature. Replace plants when they have passed their best, to keep it looking good.*

ABOVE: *Feature groups of plants in containers where the garden needs an uplift. The beach pebbles add an individual touch.*

LEFT: *Individually, these containers would not look special, but grouping them makes a focal point.*

Groups on the lawn

Clusters of pots are an ideal means to breaking up a large expanse of lawn. Don't stand them directly on the grass, but use a bed of sand or gravel – this will stand out well from the grass, and make mowing round the containers easier.

PERMANENT PLANTS FOR TUBS

It is easy to have colorful tubs and troughs in summer, but to get the best from containers you need some year-round interest. Sometimes it is worth thinking beyond the traditional summer annuals, and to reserve a few containers for permanent plants.

Small trees and shrubs give height to your patio display, and plantings that provide winter interest mean that your garden never becomes boring. Use small containers and windowboxes to add splashes of seasonal color, but include a few large tubs or troughs planted with shrubs and perennials for a more permanent display.

Many shrubs used in troughs and tubs eventually outgrow their containers. Plant these in the border and start off with new ones.

ABOVE: *This Japanese maple will eventually make an attractive small tree. In the meantime the container is an eye-catching feature.*

LEFT: *Few gardeners bother to grow herbaceous perennials in containers, but some, like this Lychnis coronaria, are brilliant in flower. If you dead-head the lychnis regularly it will remain colorful for many months.*

RIGHT: *The silver-gray cineraria in this container cannot be permanently planted in cold areas, but is easily replaced each year. Plants like this are useful for filling in the gap around the base of trees and shrubs grown as standards.*

Trees for tubs

Trees are unlikely candidates for containers, and certainly for small gardens. Fortunately the restricted root-run usually keeps them compact and they never reach the proportions of trees planted in the ground. Even in a small garden some height is useful.

Choose trees that are naturally small if possible. Laburnums, crab apples (and some of the upright-growing and compact eating apples on dwarfing roots too), *Prunus* 'Amanogawa' (a flowering cherry with narrow, upright growth), and even trees as potentially large as *Acer platanoides* 'Drummondii' (a varie-gated maple) will be happy in a large pot or tub for a number of years. Small weeping trees also look good. Try *Salix caprea* 'Pendula', *Cotoneaster* 'Hybridus Pendulus' (cascades of red berries in autumn). Even the pretty

dome-shaped gray-leaved *Pyrus salicifolia* 'Pendula' is a possibility.

These must have a heavy pot with a minimum inside diameter of 15in, and a loam-based soil mix. Even then they are likely to blow over in very strong winds unless you pack some other hefty pots around them, at least in bad weather.

Good shrubs for tubs

Camellias are perfect shrubs for tubs, combining attractive, glossy evergreen foliage with beautiful spring flowers. *Camellia* x *williamsii* and *C. japonica* hybrids are a good choice. Many rhododendrons and azaleas are also a practical proposition, and if you have a limey soil this is the best way to grow these plants . . . provided you fill the container with an ericaceous soil mix.

Many hebes make good container plants (but not for very cold or exposed areas), and there are many attractively variegated varieties. The yellow-leaved *Choisya ternata* 'Sundance' and variegated yuccas such as *Yucca filamentosa* 'Variegata' and *Y. gloriosa* 'Variegata' are also striking shrubs in containers.

For some winter interest, try *Viburnum tinus*.

Border perennials

Few people bother to grow border perennials in containers, but if you have a paved garden, or would like to introduce them to the patio, don't be afraid to experiment. Dicentras, agapanthus, and many ornamental grasses are among the plants that you might want to try, but there are very many more that you should be able to succeed with – and they will cost you nothing if you divide a plant already in the border.

Evergreen perennials

Evergreen non-woody perennials such as ajugas, bergenias and *Carex morrowii* 'Evergold' are always useful for providing color and foliage cover in the winter, but look best as part of a mixed planting.

HOW TO PLANT A TREE OR SHRUB IN A TUB

1 Choose a large tub or pot with an inside diameter of at least 15in, except for very small shrubs. Make sure it is heavy (clay or ceramic for instance, not plastic) and place pieces of broken clay pots or chipped bark over the drainage hole.

2 Part-fill with a loam-based potting soil. Do not use lightweight alternatives as the weight is required for stability.

3 Knock the plant from its pot, and if the roots are tightly wound around the root-ball, carefully tease out some of the roots so that they will grow into the surrounding potting soil more readily.

4 Test the plant for size and position. Add or remove soil as necessary, so that the top of the root-ball and soil level will be 1–2in below the rim of the pot to allow for watering.

5 Firm the soil mix around the roots, as trees and shrubs offer a great deal of wind resistance. Water thoroughly after planting, and never forget to water regularly in dry weather.

YEAR-ROUND CONTAINERS

In a large garden containers are usually used for splashes of summer color. The voids left in winter when the plants have died are not so noticeable among the many other garden features. In a small garden, and especially on a patio, bare containers in winter look positively off-putting, and only emphasize the lack of year-round plants.

The choice for summer is limitless, so the emphasis here is on autumn and winter – the seasons for which most effort has to be made.

Year-round troughs and boxes

Dwarf evergreen shrubs and dwarf conifers, in their many shapes and colors, will provide year-round interest. But to prevent them becoming so much background greenery, leave space in front to plant a few bulbs or small bedding plants. Allow for a space the size of a small pot for these seasonal plantings, so that you can easily replace the small flowers as they finish. Grow a reserve of them in pots to fit the space.

Autumn highlights

Grow one or two autumn-glory shrubs in tubs that you can bring out of their place of hiding when you need a final burst of color.

Ceratostigma willmottianum has compact growth and lovely autumn foliage tints while still producing blue flowers. Berries can also be used as a feature, and you may be able to buy compact pernettyas already bearing berries in your garden center.

Winter color

Some winter-flowering shrubs can be used in tubs, such as *Viburnum tinus* and *Mahonia* 'Charity'. But try being bold with short-term pot plants like Cape heathers (*Erica* x *hyemalis* and *E. gracilis*) and winter cherries (*Solanum capsicastrum* and similar species and hybrids). You will have to throw them away afterwards, but they will look respectable for a few weeks even in cold and frosty winter weather.

LEFT: Solanum capsicastrum *is widely sold as a houseplant in the winter months, but you can use it as a short-term plant to add a touch of color to permanent plantings of evergreens in outdoor containers. Those pictured were still happy in late winter. Discard once the berries shrivel.*
BELOW: *The intense blue flowers of* ceratostigma *last well into autumn, when there is the bonus of rich foliage color before the leaves fall.*

HOW TO PROTECT PLANTS FROM FROST

Many of the most dramatic summer patio shrubs – like daturas and oleanders – must be taken into a frost-free place for the winter. Others that are frost-tolerant but of borderline hardiness in cold areas, like the bay (*Laurus nobilis*), or that are vulnerable to frost and wind damage to the leaves that is disfiguring even though not fatal (such as *Choisya ternata* 'Sundance') need a degree of winter protection. It is a pity to lose these magnificent patio plants for the sake of a little forethought as autumn draws to a close.

A MOVING BUSINESS

Those shrubs that won't tolerate winter outdoors, even with protection, must be taken into a greenhouse or conservatory. Moving a heavy container is difficult, but the following tips are useful.

Try rolling the pot on its edge. Even a heavy container can be moved quite easily like this. Alternatively, 'walk' the container onto a low trolley. If one person pushes the trolley while another holds the container, even large trees and shrubs can be moved.

1 Shrubs that are fairly tough and need a little protection from the worst weather, can be covered with horticultural fleece, or bubble plastic. Insert four or five canes around the edge of the pot.

2 Cut the fleece or plastic to size first. If you use fleece, you may be able to buy it as a sleeve (ideal for winter protection for shrubs in tubs). Allow for an overlap over the pot.

3 If in a sleeve, slip it over the canes; if in a sheet, wrap it round the plant, allowing a generous overlap. For particularly vulnerable plants, use more than one layer.

4 Securely tie the protection around the pot. For very delicate plants, it is a good idea to bring the material well down over the pot, to keep the root-ball warm.

5 Tie the top closed if covering with fleece (moisture will be able to penetrate and tying the top will help to conserve warmth). If using plastic, it is best to leave the top open for ventilation and to permit watering if necessary.

ROCK AND WATER GARDENS

ROCK AND WATER FEATURES ADD AN EXTRA
dimension to any garden, but imagination is
needed to get the best from them in a small area.
The vast majority of rock and water plants thrive
best in a sunny position, and it may be difficult to
find a suitable site in a small garden. If you can't
find a spot that is in the sun for at least half the
day – and preferably longer – it might be better to
choose a water feature that depends less on plants
for its effect, and to grow your rock plants in
other ways, such as between paving and in raised
beds or a gravel garden.

Very small ponds are much more difficult to
'balance' biologically than large ones, and green
water is often a problem for much of the year. If
the garden is very tiny choose a bubble fountain,
wall spout, or container pond instead.

Rock gardens look best on a natural slope or built to look like a natural outcrop of rocks in a large lawn. Most small gardens offer neither opportunity. Combining a rock feature with the pond is often the most satisfactory solution. You can create the raised ground from the soil excavated for the pond.

Rock plants – or alpines if you prefer the label – offer huge scope for an enthusiastic gardener with a passion for plants but without the space to grow many. You can plant dozens in the space taken by just one medium-sized shrub, and even the tiniest garden can be home for hundreds of plants.

Be careful with the choice of water plants. Some irises and rushes are compact, others are rampant and will soon make a take-over bid. There are waterlilies that need deep water and a large surface area, others that will be happy in 9in of water and will make do with a much smaller surface area.

TOP: Sedum spurium *'Atropurpureum'*.
ABOVE: *Campanulas – here growing through* Asplenium scolopendrium – *are popular rock plants.*
RIGHT: *This sink garden contains more than half a dozen different plants in less space than a single shrub would normally occupy.*
OPPOSITE: *Raising the edges of this pond has emphasized its role as the center of attention.*
OPPOSITE ABOVE: *Various species of dianthus do well in a rock garden and always have a special appeal.*

PONDS AND WATER FEATURES

Making a pond is very easy nowadays – most flexible liners are strong and long-lasting, and pre-formed pools are as near as you can get to buying an instant pond off the shelf. If you don't have space for a 'proper' pond, make one in a barrel or shrub tub.

If you want to grow plants and keep fish, choose a bright position for your pond, one that receives sun for at least half the day. Avoid overhanging trees – they not only cast shade but shed leaves too, which can pollute the water.

Fountains and cascades

Introduce a cascade if you build a rock garden with your pond. A simple low-voltage submersible pump linking the head of the cascade with a hose is usually adequate for a small cascade with a modest flow of water.

Fountains need a large area of water, otherwise drift will cause a gradual drop in the water level. Be aware that the disturbed surface does not suit waterlilies and some other aquatic plants. A simple bubble or geyser type of jet is often more appropriate than a high, ornate jet in a small garden.

ABOVE: *You don't need a large garden to enjoy the sight and sound of moving water, as this attractive feature shows.*

Wall features

In a courtyard or a basement garden enclosed by walls, a wall fountain is often the best choice. You don't need a great gush of water.

You can fix a spout that pours water into a reservoir at the base of the wall to be recirculated through a hidden pump; alternatively buy one that is self-contained with water simply trickling into an integrated dish beneath the spout.

Miniature ponds

If you've no room for a proper pond, make one in a half-barrel or even a plastic shrub tub. Sink it into the ground, half-sink it into the soil, or have it free-standing, perhaps on a paved area such as the patio. Container ponds are not suitable for fish, but you can grow an interesting small collection of aquatic plants in them, including miniature waterlilies.

HOW TO MAKE A POND USING A LINER

1 Mark out the shape of your pond with some rope, garden hose or by sprinkling sand. Then remove the grass and excavate the soil to the required depth, leaving a shallow ledge about 9in wide at about that depth from the top.

2 Remove the grass or soil around the edge if you plan to pave it. Allow for the thickness of the paving plus a bed of mortar. Check levels and remove extra soil from one side if necessary. The water surface needs to be level to the sides of the pond.

3 Remove sharp stones and large roots, then line the pool with about ½in of damp sand – it should stick to the sides if they slope slightly. Use a polyester mat (from water garden specialists) or old carpet instead of sand if the soil is stony.

HOW TO INSTALL A PRE-FORMED POND

1 Transfer the shape of your pool to the ground by inserting canes around the edge. Use a garden hose or rope to define the shape.

2 Excavate the hole to approximately the right depth, and following the profile of the shelves as accurately as possible.

3 Place a straight-edged piece of wood across the top and check that the edges are level. Measure down to check the depths.

4 Place the pool in the hole and add or remove more soil if it does not sit snugly. Also remove any sharp stones. Check that it is absolutely straight with a carpenter's level.

5 Remove the pond and line the shape with sand. Backfill so that the pond shape fits the hole snugly.

6 Run water in from a hose, and backfill and firm again as the water rises. Check the levels frequently as the backfilling often tends to lift the pool slightly.

4 Drape the liner over the hole, anchoring the edges with bricks. Run water into the pool from a hose. As the weight of water takes the liner into the hole, release the bricks occasionally. Some creases will form but are not usually noticeable.

5 Trim the liner, leaving an overlap around the edge of about 6in, to be covered by the paving.

6 Bed the paving on mortar, covering the edge of the liner. The paving should overlap the edge of the pool by about 1in. Finish off by pointing the joints with mortar.

HOW TO PLANT A POND

The best time to plant a pond is between mid spring and early summer, when new growth is vigorous yet the plants are not too large. However, most plants can be introduced either earlier or later. Tender floaters such as *Eichhornia crassipes* and *Salvinia braziliensis* should not be introduced while there is a reasonable risk of frost.

HOW TO PLANT WATERLILIES

1 Waterlilies and other deep-water plants can be planted in the same mesh baskets used for marginal plants, but for the more vigorous waterlilies an old washing-up bowl provides more root-run. Plant as for marginals (see below).

2 Cover the soil surface with gravel. There may be space to insert a few oxygenating plants around the edge. These will probably spread and root elsewhere, but it will get them off to a good start.

3 Lower the bowl into the water. If planting early, before the leaf stalks are long, rest the bowl on a couple of bricks for a week or two, then lower to its final position. Different varieties should be planted at different depths.

HOW TO PLANT MARGINALS

1 Use a pond planting basket, and line it with a piece of burlap (sometimes sold for the purpose by water garden specialists) or a piece of horticultural fleece. Fill the container with a soil for aquatics. Insert the plant and carefully firm the soil around the roots.

2 Cover the surface with gravel. This will help to protect the soil from erosion and fish are less likely to stir it up. Gently lower the basket into the water so that it sits on the marginal shelf with about 2in of water above the soil.

Six of the best marginals
- *Caltha palustris*
Yellow flowers in spring.
- *Houttuynia cordata*
Small white flowers in summer. Green leaves with red stems, but 'Chameleon' has multicolored foliage.
- *Iris laevigata*
Mainly blue, white or pink flowers, depending on variety, in summer.
- *Juncus effusus* 'Spiralis'
Stems spirally twisted like corkscrew.
- *Pontederia cordata*
Spikes of pale blue flowers in summer and autumn.
- *Scirpus* 'Zebrinus'
Leaves transversely banded white and green.

ABOVE: *A well-planted pond has both deep-water plants like waterlilies and marginal plants around the edge.*
BELOW: Caltha palustris *is one of the easiest marginal or bog-garden plants to grow.*

Three of the best oxygenating plants

● *Elodea canadensis*
Not much to see – tightly packed small green leaves on submerged stems. Excellent oxygenator, but will require thinning out several times each season.

● *Myriophyllum* (several species)
Dense whorls of feathery green foliage that rises above the water. Can spread rapidly once established.
● *Tillaea recurva*
Bright green, almost moss-like growth just below surface.

Six of the best waterlilies for a small pond
● 'Froebelli' – Red.
● 'James Brydon' – Red.
● *Laydekeri lilacea* – Pink.
● 'Paul Hariot'
Yellow deepening to copper-red with age.
● *Pygmaea helvola*
Yellow, very small and suitable for miniature ponds.
● 'Rose Arey' – Pink.

Other deep-water aquatics
● *Aponogeton distachyos*
Slightly scented white flowers from spring to autumn.
● *Orontium aquaticum*

With a natural pond, the soil by the water's edge is usually very moist. The soil immediately behind a pre-formed or liner pool will be dry as in the rest of the garden. But there are many plants that are associated with water that will tolerate dry soil, even though they may prefer it moist. Make the most of these to give the illusion of a bog garden or natural edging to an informal pond. Plants to include are astilbes, hostas, *Iris sibirica, I. pseudacorus*, mimulus, many primulas, and hemerocallis.

Poker-like flowers with bright yellow tips in mid and late spring.

Floaters to try . . . and to avoid
Two good floaters that are unlikely to become uncontrollable are *Stratiotes aloides* and *Azolla caroliniana*. The latter spreads quickly but winter knocks it back except where winters are very mild (in cold areas it is worth overwintering a few plants in a frost-free place to start the colony again the following year).

Avoid any species of *Lemna* (duckweed). They not only spread rapidly but are very difficult to eradicate.

WAYS TO GROW ROCK PLANTS

If you have a sunny corner, a rock garden could be an attractive way to fill it. Alternatively, introduce rocks with a pond. A steeply sloped rock garden provides an opportunity to include a series of cascades that run through the rock garden to the pool beneath. It also solves the problem of what to do with the soil excavated during pond construction!

If your interests lie more with the exquisite beauty of the plants than with the landscaping aspects of a rock garden, there are plenty of ways to include alpines in areas other than a rock garden.

Combined with water

Rock gardens and ponds both require a sunny position to do well, and they associate well together. It is often possible to introduce a series of cascades linking a small pool at the top with the main pool below. Bury the connecting hose when constructing the rock garden, and use plenty of rocks to make the cascades look as natural as possible.

Very pleasing combined rock and water gardens can also be constructed without running water.

Island rock beds

Provided the lawn is reasonably large, and informal in shape, small rock outcrops can be created. You don't need many rocks for this kind of rock garden, just a few bold ones, carefully positioned so that they look as though they are protruding through the ground. For rocks to look convincing it is important to slope them into the ground, and for the strata to lie in one direction.

Rock plants in gravel gardens

Rock plants look good in gravel, so include them in a gravel garden or create a small flat gravel bed just for rock plants. Provide the same soil conditions as for a raised rockery, but on the flat. In addition, you can include a few rocks to create the impression of a scree.

Sink gardens

Alpines are perfect for sink gardens. Genuine stone sinks are ideal, but these are scarce and expensive. Perfectly attractive gardens can be created in imitation stone sinks.

Although you can simply plant 'on the flat' within the trough or sink, much more effective are 'landscaped' displays in which a section of rock face is created.

ABOVE: *If you like alpines but don't want a rock garden, why not have a whole collection of sink gardens?*
LEFT: *A low rock bank is another easy way to grow rock plants, and is also very simple to construct.*

Raised beds

The great advantage of a raised bed for alpines is that you are better able to appreciate their beauty in miniature. You can build the beds with bricks or walling blocks, but natural stone is much better, especially if you can leave plenty of planting holes in the sides.

Peat beds

The vast majority of alpines grow happily in ordinary or alkaline soil, but a few require acid conditions. If these plants appeal, build a peat bed from peat blocks, bonding the blocks like bricks. Fill with a peaty mixture or an ericaceous potting soil and plant the alpines in your chosen arrangement.

HOW TO MAKE A ROCK GARDEN

1 The base is a good place to dispose of rubble, which you can then cover with garden soil – the ideal place for soil excavated from the pond.

2 It is best to use a special soil mixture for the top 6–9in, especially if soil excavated from the pond is used. Mix together equal parts soil, coarse grit and peat (or peat substitute), and spread this evenly over the mound.

3 Lay the first rocks at the base, trying to keep the strata running in the same direction.

4 Lever the next row of rocks into position. Use rollers and levers to move them.

5 As each layer is built up, add more of the soil mixture, and consolidate it around the rocks.

6 Ensure that the sides all slope inwards, and make the top reasonably flat rather than building it into a pinnacle. Position the plants, then cover the exposed soil with a thin layer of horticultural grit.

CHOOSING AND PLANTING

A visit to any garden center will reveal a choice selection of plants for your rock garden. One of the delights of collecting alpines is the constant surprises as new treasures are encountered, and the ability to indulge in a wide range of plants that won't take up much space.

The plants suggested here can only be an arbitrary selection of some of the best, with the emphasis on plants that are fairly widely available.

Useful for a wall
- *Acaena microphylla* (top or face)
- *Achillea tomentosa* (top)
- *Alyssum montanum* (top)
- *Arabis caucasica* (top or face)
- *Arenaria balearica* (top or face)
- *Aubrieta* (face)
- *Aurinia saxatilis* (top or face)
- *Campanula garganica* (face)
- *Cerastium tomentosum* (face)
- *Corydalis lutea* (face)
- *Dianthus deltoides* (top or face)
- *Erinus alpinus* (top or face)
- *Gypsophila repens* (top or face)
- *Sedum,* many (face)
- *Sempervivum,* many (face)

Try these in a trough
- *Arabis ferdinandi-coburgi* 'Variegata'
- *Aster alpinus*
- *Gentiana acaulis*
- *Hypericum olympicum*
- *Phlox douglasii*
- *Potentilla tabernaemontani*
- *Raoulia australis*
- *Rhodohypoxis baurii*
- *Sedum lydium*
- *Sempervivum* (various)

Good starter plants for a rock garden
Some of these plants are quite rampant or large – *Aurinia saxatilis* and helianthemums, for example. If you are not familiar with particular plants, look them up in an encyclopedia.

- *Acaena microphylla*
- *Antennaria dioica* 'Rosea'

- *Arabis ferdinandi-coburgi* 'Variegata'
- *Armeria maritima*
- *Aurinia saxatilis*
- *Campanula carpatica*
- *Campanula cochleariifolia*
- *Dianthus deltoides*
- *Dryas octopetala*

- *Erinus alpinus*
- *Gentiana acaulis*
- *Gentiana septemfida*
- *Gentiana sino-ornata*
- *Geranium subcaulescens* 'Splendens'
- *Gypsophila repens*
- *Helianthemum*

LEFT: Aurinia saxatilis.

BELOW LEFT: Dianthus deltoides *'Electra'*.
BELOW: Helianthemum *'Fire Dragon'*.

- *Hypericum olypicum*
- *Iberis sempervirens* 'Snowflake'
- *Oxalis adenophylla*
- *Phlox douglasii*
- *Phlox subulata*
- *Pulsatilla vulgaris*
- *Raoulia australis*
- *Saxifraga* (mossy type)
- *Sedum spathulifolium* 'Cape Blanco'
- *Sedum spurium*
- *Sempervivum* (various)
- *Silene schafta*
- *Thymus serpyllum* (various)
- *Veronica prostrata*

LEFT: Sempervivum ballsii.

HOW TO PLANT ALPINES

1 Position the plants while still in their pots so that you can see how they look and can move them around easily if necessary.

2 Use a trowel to take out a hole a little larger than the root-ball. You can buy narrow trowels that are particularly useful for planting in the crevices between rocks.

3 Make sure the plant is at the correct depth, then trickle gritty soil around the roots and firm it well.

4 Finish off by covering the exposed surface with more grit.

CHOOSING PLANTS

Hard landscaping (paving, walls, fences, pergolas, and so on)
is what gives a garden a strong sense of design, and provides the skeleton
that gives the garden its shape. But it is the soft landscaping – the plants –
that provides the flesh, shape and texture of the garden.
The same basic design can look very different in the hands of
gardeners with different ideas on the use of plants.

ABOVE: *Mixing different types of plant can*
be very effective. This border contains shrubs,
herbaceous plants, bulbs, and grasses.

OPPOSITE: *No matter how attractive the*
design of a garden, it is the plants
that make it pretty.

BEDS AND BORDERS

BEDS AND BORDERS NEED TO BE PLANNED. THE shape will affect the overall appearance, of course, but there are also practical considerations such as the amount of maintenance required, the theme to be created, as well as the crucial question of the actual plants to be used.

Formal beds and borders are normally dictated by the basic design concept, which will often determine the type of plants you can use. A formal rose garden will clearly feature roses, and only the 'filler' plants might have to be debated. A classic style with neat asymmetrical beds cut

into the lawn, or edged by clipped box, demands the type of formal bedding associated with this type of garden.

Herbaceous and shrub borders are much more open to interpretation, and the actual plants used will have as much effect on the overall impression created as the shape or size of the border.

In traditional large gardens there is a clear distinction between herbaceous borders and shrub borders, but few small gardens can afford this luxury and the inclusion of a 'mixed border' is the usual compromise. Here shrubs jostle for

LEFT: *By curving the corners of borders in a small garden you can generate extra planting space that helps to make the garden more interesting.*

OPPOSITE ABOVE: *A garden like this, with plenty of shrubs such as roses, require little maintenance and because the hard landscaping is minimal is relatively inexpensive to create.*

OPPOSITE BELOW: *Single-sided herbaceous borders can look right in a rural setting if you have enough space. A border like this can be colorful for many months.*

position with herbaceous plants and annuals, while summer bedding plants and spring bulbs make bids for any areas of inhabitable space left. There is nothing wrong with this type of gardening: the border looks clothed long after the herbaceous plants have died down, and there will be flowers and pockets of changing interest for a much longer period than could be achieved with shrubs alone.

Color themes are also difficult to achieve in a small garden, and although single-color borders can be planted in a small garden, it is best to be a little more flexible. Settle for a 'golden corner' rather than a golden border, or a blue-and-silver theme for just part of a border rather than a more extensive area.

Small beds cut into the lawn do not have to be filled with summer bedding and then replaced by spring bulbs and spring bedding. Instead plant them with blocks of perennial ground cover, or use a perennial edging and plant seasonal flowers within it.

ISLAND BEDS

Traditionally, low-growing seasonal plants have been grown in beds cut into the lawn – island beds – and taller herbaceous plants and shrubs placed in long borders designed to be viewed from one side. Island beds planted with herbaceous plants and shrubs bridge this divide, and provide planting opportunities that can be put to good use in a small garden.

Planting principles

Island beds are intended to be viewed from all sides, so the tallest plants usually go in the center and the smaller ones around the edge. Don't be too rigid, however. Concentrate on creating a bed that you have to walk around to see the other side, rather than simply planting tall summer flowers like delphiniums in the center. Shrubby plants, even medium-sized evergreens, might be better for the center of the bed, with other lower-growing shrubs creating bays that can be filled with plants that die down for the winter. Your bed will then retain its function of breaking up a lawn and creating a

diversion that has to be explored.

Don't be afraid to plant a small tree, such as *Malus floribunda*, in an island bed, to create much-needed height.

If seasonal bedding appeals more than shrubs and border perennials, then island beds can still be used creatively for these.

The question of shape

Most people think of island beds as informal in outline, but you can introduce rectangular beds if this suits the style of your garden.

Curved beds generally look much more pleasing, however, especially if you introduce broad and narrow areas so that there are gentle bays.

Design considerations

Use an island bed to break the line of sight. By taking it across the garden, an island bed may distract attention from an uninspiring view – whether beyond the garden or simply the fence itself. Attention is directed to the sides, and as you walk around the bed, the eye is taken into the bed rather than to the perimeters.

A series of island beds can be used to divide up a long, narrow garden. Instead of the eye being taken in a straight line to the end, the beds become a series of diversions.

BELOW: *Island beds help to break up a large lawn, and create a sense of height.*

ONE-SIDED BORDERS

Single-sided borders are useful if you want to create flowery boundaries around the perimeter and emphasize an open space within the garden, turning the garden in on itself. These borders are also useful for taking the eye to a distant focal point, and, by varying the width of the border, you can create a false sense of perspective that can appear to alter the size of the garden.

Straight and narrow beds

Most gardens have at least some straight and narrow borders around the edge of the lawn, a favorite spot for roses or seasonal bedding. If you want to cut down on the regular replanting work, plant with dwarf shrubs as backbone plants, then include flowering ground cover herbaceous plants such as hardy geraniums and spring bulbs to provide flowers over a long period.

Make a border look wider by laying a mowing edge. Then use plants that will sprawl over the edge, softening the hard line and giving the impression of a wider border.

The advantages of curved borders

Straight edges are easier to mow and trim, but unless the border is wide and variation is created with the use of shrubs of various sizes, they can appear unimaginative and may take the eye too quickly along the garden, making it seem smaller. Gentle curves that create bays enable the plants to be brought further out into the garden and provide much more adventurous planting scope.

It may be possible to modify an existing straight border by cutting into the lawn. Bear in mind that mowing time is likely to be increased rather than decreased, however.

ABOVE: *Single-sided borders are the best choice for small town gardens that have high enclosing walls, especially if you can use climbers or tall plants to hide the wall.*
LEFT: *A single-sided mixed border.*

Turning corners

Don't forget that borders can turn corners. Right-angled turns seldom look satisfactory, however, so add a curve to the corner. This will give it greater depth at that point.

You can even take the border right round the garden in a continuous strip. A small square garden with a circular central lawn surrounded by border can look quite spectacular if well planted with a wide range of plants that hold interest throughout the seasons.

HOW TO MAKE BEDS AND BORDERS

If you are making a garden from scratch, areas allocated to lawns, beds and borders will be laid out accordingly, but you can often improve an existing garden by altering the shape of a border, or creating beds in what is currently a large and uninspiring lawn.

HOW TO MARK OUT AN OVAL BED

For small formal beds, such as ovals and circles, it is best to sow or lay the grass over the whole area first, then cut out the beds once the grass has become established.

Start by marking out a rectangle that will contain the oval. Afterwards you can check that it is square by measuring across the diagonals, which should be the same length.

Place a peg half way along each side, and stretch a string between them. The two strings will cross at the center point. Then cut a piece of string half the *length* of the oval and using a side peg as a pivot, insert pegs where it intersects the long string along the center.

Make a loop from a piece of string twice the distance between one of these two pegs and the top or bottom of the oval (whichever is the furthest away).

With the loop draped over the inner pegs, scribe a line in the grass while keeping the string taut. You can make the line more visible by using a narrow-necked bottle filled with dry sand instead of a stick.

Use an edging iron to cut out the shape, then lift the grass with a spade.

HOW TO MAKE A CURVED BORDER

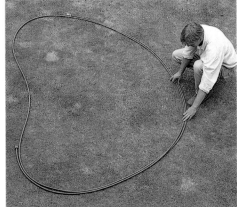

1 If you want a quick and easy method, and can trust your eye for an even curve, lay garden hose where you think the new edge should be. Run warm water through it first if the weather is cold, otherwise it may not be flexible enough to lie on the ground without awkward kinks.

2 The best way to judge whether the curves are satisfactory is to view the garden from an upstairs window, and have someone on the ground who can make further adjustments if necessary.

3 When the profile is satisfactory, run sand along the marker (dry sand in a wine bottle is a convenient method). Use an edging iron to cut the new edge, then lift the surplus grass and dig the soil thoroughly before attempting to replant.

4 An alternative and a more accurate way to achieve smooth curves is to use a stick or bottle fixed to a string attached to a peg. Use this as a pivot. By adjusting the length of the string and the position of the pivot, a series of curves can be achieved. Cut the edge as before.

HOW TO GET A NEAT EDGE

Emphasize the profile of your beds and borders, as well as your paths, by giving them a crisp or interesting edge. A mowing edge is a practical solution for a straight-edged border. Curved beds and borders usually have to be edged in other ways.

Some methods, like the corrugated edging strip and the wooden edge shown below are not particularly elegant, but they help to prevent the gradual erosion of the lawn through constant trimming and cutting back, and they maintain a crisp profile.

Using ornate or unusual edgings

For a period garden, choose a suitable edging. Victorian-style rope edging tiles are appropriate. If you live in a coastal area, consider using large seashells. If you enjoy your wine as well as your garden, why not put the empty bottles to use by forming an edging with them? Bury them neck-down in a single or double row, with just a portion showing.

TOP: *It is possible to buy a modern version of Victorian rope-edging.*
ABOVE: *Edgings such as this are useful if you want to create a formal or old-fashioned effect.*

HOW TO FIT EDGING STRIPS

Edging strips like this are available in a thin metal, soft enough to cut with old scissors, or in plastic. These strips help stop erosion of the grass through frequent edge clipping and cutting back. Although these may not be the most decorative edging strips, they are quick and easy to fit.

1 Make a slit trench along the lawn edge with a spade, then lay the strip alongside the trench and cut to length. Place the edging strip loosely into it.

2 Backfill with soil for a firm fit. Press the strip in gently as you proceed. Finish off by tapping it level with a hammer over a straight-edged piece of wood.

HOW TO FIT WOODEN EDGING ROLL

Wired rolls of sawn logs can make a strong and attractive edging where you want the bed to be raised slightly above the lawn, but bear in mind that it may be difficult to mow right up to the edge.

1 Cut the roll to length using wire-cutters or strong pliers to cut through the wires, and insert the edging in a shallow trench. Join pieces by wiring them together. Backfill with soil for a firm fit. Make sure that the edging is level, first by eye. Use a hammer over a straight-edged piece of wood to tap it down. Then check the height with a carpenter's level. Adjust as necessary.

PLANNING BORDERS

THE SECRET OF A SUCCESSFUL BORDER IS PLANNING for a long period of interest. However large a border, it probably will not remain attractive for more than about a month if you plan it only with plants that flower together. Planning should include not only plants that make pleasing associations when flowering, but that look good even out of bloom. Also incorporate plants that flower at different seasons.

The risk of planting a series of plants that bloom at different times is an uncoordinated appearance, with plants in flower dotted about amid a swathe of foliage in varying stages of

ABOVE: *Hydrangeas look good in shrub borders or mixed borders, but the flower color may vary according to the acidity or alkalinity of the soil.*

LEFT: *Don't be afraid to use a focal point like a birdbath in a border. It will be eyecatching even when the plants are not at their best.*

growth. Sadly, in a small garden there isn't space to devote to a spring border, summer border, and autumn border.

Some of these shortcomings can be overcome by planting a mixed border that clearly incorporates many different kinds of plants, and by always planting in bold groups rather than using isolated specimens.

If starting from scratch, plan your borders on paper first. In an existing border you will obviously want to retain as many plants as possible, but be prepared to uproot and move or discard those that are out of place.

Choosing plants is always exciting, and in the following pages you will find suggestions of some of the most useful for a small garden. Space precludes mention of more than a small selection of suitable plants, so add special favorites and others that suit *your* garden and *your* taste.

TOP: *A border showing a good mix of shrubs and perennials.*
ABOVE: *Hollies are useful for the back of a shrub border.*

HOW TO PLANT A BORDER

You don't have to be an artist to draw a functional planting plan. You can buy simple computer programs that will help you draw one up, but you still have to provide the plant knowledge that makes a border come alive and fulfil your own expectations. You can achieve results that are just as acceptable, and probably just as quickly, with pencil and paper.

A SCALE OUTLINE

1 Draw the outline shape of the bed and border, marking on the scale. Use graph paper so that you can easily estimate the size of a particular plant as you work.

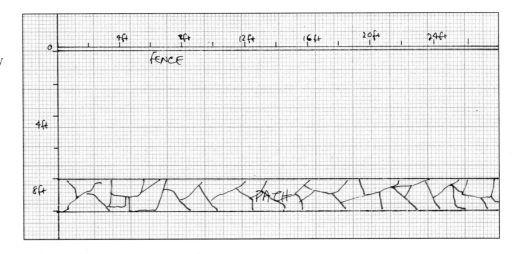

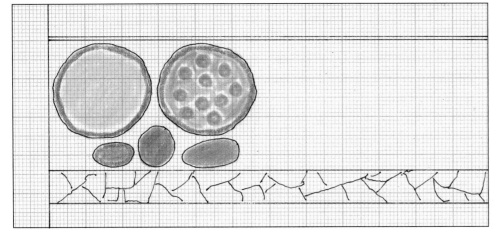

2 Make a list of plants that you want to include. Be sure to add essential details such as height, spread, and flowering season. If you find it easier to move around pieces of paper rather than use pencil and eraser initially, cut out several pieces of paper of appropriate size, with the height and flowering period marked on. You could color them – evergreen greens, variegated green and gold stripes, and flowering plants in the color of the blooms.

3 Either start with a basic plan with a series of spaces to be allocated (just indicate whether tall, medium or small), or shuffle around your cut-outs until they appear to form a pleasing pattern. Don't worry about whether the plants will fill the exact shape – with time they will all grow into each other, and in the meantime you can fill the gaps with annuals.

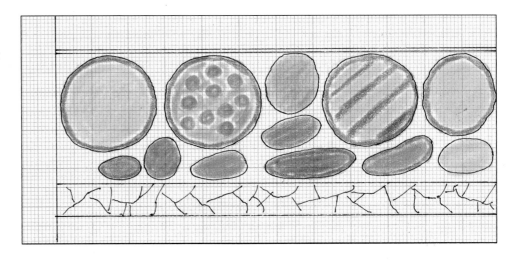

4 When satisfied with your key plants, draw these in on a more detailed planting plan. Then fill in the gaps with other plants, not necessarily on your priority list.

If you feel sufficiently artistically inclined, you can try a profile view that will give a better idea of how the border will look – though you can only make a snapshot of how it would look in one season.

HOW TO PLANT HERBACEOUS PLANTS

GUIDELINES TO GETTING IT RIGHT

- Unless the plants are large, plant in groups of about three – a bold spash usually looks better than single plants. Using single plants just because space is limited is a common mistake – the impact is often better if you use fewer kinds but more of each.
- Take into account the likely ultimate height, but remember that plants may grow taller in one garden than another.
- As a rule place the taller plants at the back (in the center of an island bed), with the smallest at the front. But don't follow this too slavishly unless planting formal summer bedding. A few focal point plants that stand out from the rest can be very effective.
- Consider planting the border so that different parts are at their best at different times, perhaps starting with spring flowers at one end and working through to autumn at the other.
- Use foliage plants to maintain interest throughout the border.

1 Always prepare the soil first. Dig it deeply, remove weeds, and incorporate a fertilizer and garden compost if impoverished. Most herbaceous plants are sold in pots, so space them out according to your plan. Change positions if associations don't look right.

2 Water thoroughly about half an hour before knocking the plant from its pot, then remove a planting hole with a trowel. If the roots are wound tightly around the root-ball, carefully tease out a few of them first. Work methodically from the back of the border, or from one end.

3 Firm the soil around the roots to remove any large pockets of air.

4 Always water thoroughly after planting, and keep well watered in dry weather for the first few months.

PLANTING FOR TEXTURE

Quite dramatic plantings can be achieved simply by planting blocks of the same plant – whether summer bedding, herbaceous perennials or shrubs. If the garden is seen as an area of voids and masses, blocks of colors and textures, the overall impression can be as important as individual plants. Ground cover plants are ideal for this purpose.

ABOVE: *Thyme is a useful ground cover for a sunny position, and will even tolerate being walked upon occasionally.*

CONVENTIONAL PLANTING

Many ground cover plants spread by sideways growth, sending up new plants a short distance from the parent. These are best planted like normal herbaceous or shrubby plants. Suppress weeds initially with a 2in layer of a mulch such as chipped bark. This is also the best way to plant any kind of ground cover that forms part of a mixed border.

HOW TO PLANT GROUND COVER

If planting ground cover plants as a 'texture block', or perhaps to cover an area of ground that is difficult to cultivate, such as a steep slope, it is best to plant through a mulching sheet. You can use black sheet plastic, but a proper mulching sheet is better as it allows water to penetrate. However, do not use the sheet method for plants that colonize by spreading shoots that send up new plants, as the sheet will prevent growth by suppressing the shoots as effectively as the weeds.

1 Prepare the ground well, eliminating weeds. Add rotted manure or garden compost, and rake in fertilizer if the soil is impoverished.
  Secure the sheet around each edge. Tuck the edges firmly into the ground and cover with soil. Make two slits in the form of a cross where you want to plant.

2 Plant through the sheet as you would normally, firming the soil around the roots.
  If you use small plants, planting with a trowel will not be a problem. Water thoroughly.

3 Although the mulching sheet will suppress weeds very effectively while the ground cover is still young and not able to do the job itself, it does not look attractive, so cover it with an ornamental mulch, such as chipped bark.

HOW TO PLANT SHRUBS

1 Most shrubs are sold in pots, and can be planted at any time of the year when the ground is not frozen or waterlogged. Space them out in their pots first, then adjust if the spacing does not look even.

2 Prepare the ground thoroughly, making sure it is free of weeds. Dig in plenty of organic material such as well-rotted manure or garden compost. Otherwise use a purchased planting mix.

3 Excavate the hole and try the plant for size. Use a garden cane or piece of wood across the hole to make sure the plant is at its original depth. Add or remove soil as necessary.

4 Remove the plant from the pot. If the roots are tightly wound around the root-ball, carefully tease some of them free, to encourage rapid rooting.

5 Firm the plant in well to eliminate large air pockets. Gentle pressure with the heel is an efficient way to do this, or alternatively you can do this by hand.

6 Rake or hoe in a balanced fertilizer to get the plant off to a good start. In autumn use one that is slow acting or has controlled release, to avoid stimulating growth during the cold months. If planting in winter, wait until spring before adding the fertilizer. Water well, then mulch with a 2in layer of organic material such as garden compost, cocoa shells, or chipped bark.

COLOR THEMES

Color themes can be very effective, and although it may not be practical to plant whole borders like this in a small garden, you can often use a color theme in part of a border, devote an island bed to shades of one or two colors, or perhaps cheer up a dull corner with yellow and gold.

Mixed borders

The plants suggested here will form the foundation of a color theme for a mixed border, but you can add to them and broaden the scope by using bulbs and annuals in appropriate colors too.

Red borders are best avoided in a small garden. They need space and the relief of contrasting colors to be at their most effective.

Blue and silver

Agapanthus hybrids
Deciduous to evergreen perennial. Light to deep blue ball-shaped flower heads from mid and late summer *18 × 30in.*

Artemisia absinthium
Deciduous sub-shrub. Deeply divided silvery-gray leaves. Yellow flowers in mid and late summer *3 × 2ft.*

Artemisia ludoviciana
Herbaceous perennial. Silver-gray foliage *3ft × 18in.*

Ceanothus x *burkwoodii*
Evergreen shrub. Clusters of bright blue flowers mid summer to mid autumn *8 × 7ft.*

Delphinium hybrids
Herbaceous perennial. Tall flower spikes in various shades of blue *6 × 2ft.*

Festuca glauca
Grass. Dense tufts of blue-gray leaves *9 × 9in.*

Hibiscus syriacus 'Blue Bird'
Deciduous shrub. Lilac-blue flowers appearing from late summer to mid autumn *8 × 8ft.*

Nepeta x *faassenii*
Herbaceous perennial. Spike-like heads of lavender-blue flowers all summer. Gray-green leaves *18 × 18in.*

Perovskia atriplicifolia
Shrubby perennial. Feathery sprays of violet-blue flowers in late summer and early autumn. Gray-green leaves *4ft × 18in.*

LEFT: *Many ceanothus grow tall, so use them where you need bold plants for the back of a blue border. There are both evergreen and deciduous kinds of ceanothus.*

BELOW LEFT: *Gray-leaved plants are useful for filling in between blue flowers. This one is* Artemisia ludoviciana.

ABOVE: *Delphiniums are some of the best blue herbaceous border plants.*

Santolina chamaecyparissus
Evergreen shrub. Silvery, woolly leaves on mound-forming plant. Small yellow flowers in mid summer *18 × 18in.*

Senecio 'Sunshine' (syn. *Brachyglottis* 'Sunshine')
Evergreen shrub. Silver-gray foliage. Yellow daisy-type flowers in mid and late summer *3 × 4ft.*

Stachys lanata (syn. *S. byzantina* or *S. olympica*)
Almost evergreen herbaceous perennial. Bold silvery leaves. Spikes of purple flowers in mid summer *12 × 12in.*

Yellow and gold

Achillea filipendulina
Herbaceous perennial. Flat heads of lemon-yellow flowers in mid and late summer *3 × 3ft.*

Anthemis tinctoria
Herbaceous perennial. Yellow daisy-like flowers early to late summer. 'E. C. Buxton' is lemon-yellow, 'Grallagh Gold' is deep golden-yellow *2½ft × 18in.*

Aurinia saxatilis
Evergreen shrubby perennial. Golden-yellow flowers in mid and late spring. Gray-green leaves *12 × 18in.*

ABOVE: Achillea filipendulina *'Gold Plate', one of the essential plants for a yellow border.*

Berberis thunbergii 'Aurea'
Deciduous shrub. Yellow foliage, with pale yellow flowers in mid spring. Red berries in autumn *4 × 4ft.*

Choisya ternata 'Sundance'
Evergreen shrub that is generally planted in a somewhat sheltered position). Yellow foliage. White flowers in mid and late spring *5 × 5ft.*

Forsythia x *intermedia*
Deciduous shrub. Covered with yellow flowers in early and mid spring *8 × 7ft.*

Hemerocallis hybrids
Herbaceous perennial. There are many yellow varieties, flowering throughout summer *3 × 2½ft.*

Hypericum 'Hidcote'
Evergreen or semi-evergreen shrub. Large yellow flowers from mid summer to early autumn *5 × 5ft.*

Ligustrum ovalifolium 'Aureum'
Evergreen or semi-evergreen shrub. Green and gold foliage *8 × 8ft,* but can be clipped to keep it more compact if desired.

LEFT: Hypericum calycinum *can be a rampant partner for other plants, but use it wherever you need to create a bold splash of yellow in an unpromising position.*

BELOW: *Hemerocallis come in a range of colors, but there are many good yellow varieties, such as 'Dutch Beauty'.*

Lonicera nitida 'Baggesen's Gold'
Evergreen shrub. Golden foliage *4 × 6ft.*

Philadelphus coronarius 'Aureus'
Deciduous shrub. Yellow leaves (can become scorched in strong sun; turn green by late summer). White flowers in late spring and early summer *8 × 6ft.*

Potentilla fruticosa
Deciduous shrub. Many varieties with yellow flowers all summer *4 × 4ft.*

Solidago hybrids
Herbaceous perennial. Sprays of bright yellow flowers in late summer and early autumn *12in–5ft × 12in–2ft,* according to the variety selected.

EVERBRIGHT EVERGREENS

Evergreens alone can make a dull garden. They need to be relieved by plants that renew themselves, otherwise you miss the variety that comes with fresh green leaves newly emerged from their buds or the final fling of many shrubs as they go out in a blaze of colorful glory in the autumn. But a garden without evergreens is equally dull, and the clever use of them will ensure that your garden always looks good, whatever the season.

Use a few evergreens in mixed borders and beds, so that there is some height and texture in winter, or devote an area of the garden to evergreens – a heather and dwarf conifer garden can look superb. Try evergreens for focal points and specimen trees in the lawn.

When creating an evergreen bed or border, use plants in many different shades of green, and use variegated plants between plain ones.

Aucuba japonica
Large, glossy leaves. Flowers generally insignificant, but red berries sometimes a bonus. Choose one of the variegated varieties
6 × 6ft.

Berberis darwinii
Small, holly-shaped leaves. Masses of attractive small orange-yellow flowers in mid and late spring
8 × 8ft.

Bergenia hybrids
Evergreen non-woody perennial, useful as ground cover in front of shrubs. Large, rounded leaves, often tinged red or purple in winter. Pink, red or white flowers in spring
1 × 2ft.

Camellia hybrids
Glossy leaves and large single or double flowers, usually in shades of pink, red or white, in spring
8 × 6ft.

Ceanothus x '*burkwoodii*'
See *Color themes.*

Choisya ternata '*Sundance*'
See *Color themes.*

ABOVE: Erica carnea '*Myretoun Ruby*' is just one of many attractive winter-flowering plants.

OPPOSITE: *Hebes are excellent compact, rounded plants (though some are tall). This is* Hebe × franciscana '*Variegata*', *suitable for even the tiniest plot.*

LEFT: *Evergreens have the advantage of looking good all year, like this combination of* Elaeagnus pungens '*Maculata*' *with* Hebe pinguifolia '*Pagei*' *in front.*

Cotoneaster dammeri
Prostrate ground cover to use in front of other shrubs. Small leaves. White flowers in early summer, red berries during the autumn and winter *2–3in × 5ft.*

Elaeagnus pungens 'Maculata'
Green leaves boldly splashed with gold in the center. Very striking in winter sun *8 × 8ft.*

Erica
There are many species and varieties – look especially for varieties of *Erica carnea* (syn. *E. herbacea*) and *E.* x *darleyensis*, both winter-flowering and lime-tolerant *1 × 2ft.*

Escallonia macrantha
Small leaves, clusters of pink or red flowers during the summer *6 × 6ft.*

Euonymus fortunei
Will grow along the ground or up against a wall. Choose one of the variegated varieties, such as 'Emerald 'n' Gold' (green and gold) *1 × 4ft* on the ground.

Hebe
Hebes make nicely shaped, usually rounded, plants and often have attractive flowers and sometimes colorful or variegated foliage. Heights can range from *1–4ft*, with similar spreads, depending on species. Many are of borderline hardiness where frosts can be severe, so check with your local garden center to see which ones are reliable enough for your area.

Ilex
The holly needs little introduction, but for a small garden choose one trained as a bush and a variegated variety such as 'Golden King' or 'Golden Queen' (the King is female and has berries, the Queen is male and doesn't!) *10 × 8ft.*

Lonicera nitida 'Baggesen's Gold'
See *Color themes.*

Mahonia 'Charity'
Fragrant clusters of yellow flowers throughout early and mid winter *8 × 6ft.*

Phormium hybrids
Tall, sword-shaped leaves arising from ground level. Usually variegated cream or shades of pink or purple, according to variety. Of borderline hardiness in areas where frosts can be severe, so check with your local garden center about which ones are suitable for your garden *4–6ft × 3–4ft.*

Rosmarinus officinalis
Gray-green, aromatic leaves. Small blue flowers during the spring *6 × 5ft.*

Santolina chamaecyparissus
See *Color themes.*

Senecio 'Sunshine'
See *Color themes.*

BELOW: *Rosemary is pretty in flower, and in mild areas will often start blooming in late winter.*
LEFT: *Hollies are usually so slow-growing that most people can find space for one. This one is* Ilex aquifolium *'Aurea Marginata'.*

Viburnum tinus
Deep to mid green leaves on tidy bush. White flowers (tinged pink in some varieties) from late autumn to early spring *8 × 6ft.*

Yucca filamentosa 'Variegata'
Sword-like leaves with broad cream and yellow margins. Large bell-shaped flowers on tall spikes in mid and late summer *4 × 3ft.*

DWARF CONIFERS

A good garden center will have hundreds of dwarf conifers, in a wide range of shades, shapes, and sizes. The permutations are enormous, and the best way to choose them is to go along armed with a book or catalog that will give you likely sizes after, say, 15 years, then choose combinations that will make a pleasing group.

COLOR FOR THE COLD MONTHS

Evergreens provide winter clothes for the garden, but they don't look very dressy and they are best interspersed with plants that renew themselves. There is no substitute for flowers and fruits, which, though more transient, are all the more appreciated.

Autumn leaf color can be as bold and bright as many flowers, but it is worth including some autumn blooms too. A few well-placed pools of late flowers will prolong summer and keep autumn at bay.

Don't overlook colorful barks and twigs in winter, which can become focal points on a sunny day.

Chimonanthus praecox
Deciduous shrub. Scented yellow flowers on bare stems in winter *8 × 8ft.*

Chrysanthemum
Look for varieties that flower late. Some flower well into late autumn and even early winter. Height varies with variety. Consult a specialist book or ask your garden center for suitable varieties.

Colchicum speciosum and hybrids
Corms with large crocus-like flowers, mainly in shades of pink and mauve, single or double, in autumn. The foliage does not appear until spring *6 × 9in.* The leaves can double the height.

Cornus mas
Deciduous shrub or small tree. Masses of tiny yellow flowers on bare branches in late winter and early spring *10 × 8ft.*

Crocus speciosus
Corm. Lilac-blue typical crocus flowers during the autumn *4 × 3in.*

Crocus tommasinianus
Corm, flowering between mid winter and early spring. Typical crocus flowers, usually lilac or purple in color *3 × 3in.*

Cyclamen coum
Corm. Miniature cyclamen-shaped flowers with reflexed petals. Mainly shades of pink, but also white. Flowers early winter to early spring. Leaves frequently marbled silver *3 × 6in.*

Cyclamen hederifolium (syn. *C. neapolitanum*).
Similar to above but flowers from late summer to late autumn.

Erica
See *Everbright evergreens*.

Hamamelis mollis
Fragrant spidery yellow flowers on bare branches in mid and late winter *8 × 8ft.*

ABOVE: *Chrysanthemum 'Ruby Mould'.*

LEFT: *Long before spring crocuses are in flower, the blooms of* C. tommasinianus *will be putting in an appearance. These were photographed in late winter.*

Helleborus niger
Evergreen perennial border plant. Large white flowers in mid winter *12 × 18in.*

Helleborus orientalis
Evergreen perennial border plant. Large white, pink, or purple flowers in late winter and early spring *18in × 2ft.*

Iris unguicularis (syn. *I. stylosa*)
Evergreen perennial border plant. Large blue iris flowers in winter and early spring *12 × 18in.*

Jasminum nudiflorum
Sprawling shrub, usually grown against a wall or trellis. Bright yellow flowers from late autumn to early spring *8 × 8ft.*

Mahonia 'Charity'
See *Everbright evergreens.*

Nerine bowdenii
Heads of pretty pink, spidery flowers on leafless stems from late summer to early winter. The foliage appears in spring *2 × 1ft.*

Prunus subhirtella 'Pendula' (syn. 'Autumnalis Pendula')
Small to medium-sized drooping deciduous tree. White flowers, sometimes tinged pink, from late autumn and throughout the winter in mild spells *10 × 10ft.*

Sternbergia lutea
Bulb. Crocus-like yellow flowers in mid and late autumn *4 × 4in.*

Viburnum x *bodnantense* 'Dawn'
Deciduous shrub. Small clusters of white to pink flowers on bare stems from late autumn to early spring *8 × 5ft.*

Viburnum tinus
See *Everbright evergreens.*

LEFT ABOVE: *The hellebores span winter and spring. This is* H. orientalis guttatus.
LEFT: Iris unguicularis *can be in bloom in mild spells right through the winter. The plants take a few years to settle down before flowering prolifically.*
BELOW: Nerine bowdenii *flowers in autumn, but will continue into winter.*

COLORFUL STEMS

A specimen tree with attractive bark, perhaps placed in a lawn or in an open position and surrounded by winter-flowering heathers, can be a winter focal point. One of the white-bark birches such as *Betula jacquemontii* always looks good. If you need a really small tree, however, try *B. pendula* 'Youngii', a small weeping tree.

In a small garden, shrubs are more likely to be a practical proposition, and two of the best are *Cornus alba* 'Sibirica' (red stems) and *C. stolonifera* 'Flaviramea' (green stems).

As a half-way house between tree and shrub, pollard *Salix alba* 'Chermesina', a willow with scarlet shoots. Cut the stems hard back to a stump perhaps 4ft tall; you will need to do this every second year.

AUTUMN LEAVES AND BERRIES

Autumn tints will provide a few extra weeks of border color at a time when every bit of interest in the garden is appreciated. Berries also add a dash of spice, and some of them will remain for many months, even through to spring in a mild winter when the birds leave them alone.

Amelanchier laevis
A small deciduous tree or large shrub. Masses of white flowers in spring, sometimes black berries in summer, rich autumn foliage color. *A. lamarckii* is very similar to *A. laevis* 10 × 8ft.

Berberis thunbergii
Deciduous shrub. Yellow flowers throughout the spring, scarlet berries and brilliant red autumn foliage 4 × 5ft.

Berberis wilsoniae
Deciduous shrub. Small yellow flowers in mid summer, coral red berries and red and orange foliage in autumn 3 × 4ft.

Ceratostigma plumbaginoides
Deciduous sub-shrub. Clusters of small blue flowers appear from mid summer to late autumn. Leaves turn a beautiful red in autumn 12 × 18in.

Clerodendrum trichotomum
Large deciduous shrub. Starry white fragrant flowers in late summer, followed by blue berries in crimson calyces in early and mid autumn 8 × 7ft.

Cornus alba
Deciduous suckering shrub. Attractive autumn foliage coloring, then red stems throughout the winter 7 × 7ft.

Cotoneaster horizontalis
Deciduous, ground-hugging shrub for front of border (can also be used against a fence or wall). Small pink flowers in early summer, followed by red berries later. Bright red foliage tints throughout the autumn 2 × 6ft.

ABOVE: *The amelanchiers are usually grown for their white flowers in spring, but they have a second burst of color when the leaves turn. This species is A. laevis.*

LEFT: Cornus alba *is an excellent shrub. After the brief spell of glory as the leaves color before they fall, there is the winter-long attraction of red stems.*

Fothergilla major
Deciduous shrub. Dark green leaves, orange-yellow or red before they fall. Scented white flowers in late spring 6 × 5ft.

Ilex
See *Everbright evergreens*.

Malus 'John Downie'
Small to medium-sized deciduous tree. White apple blossom in late spring. Conical yellow and crimson crab apples produced in autumn 20 × 8ft.

Malus tschonoskii
Deciduous tree, which though tall is a candidate for a small garden by virtue of its slender, pencil-like profile. White blossom tinged pink in late spring. Dull red fruits flushed yellow (not a feature). Red and yellow autumn foliage 20 × 7ft.

Pernettya mucronata
Evergreen shrub. Small, sharply pointed glossy leaves. Inconspicuous white flowers in late spring. Clusters of berries – shades of pink, red, purple and white, according to variety – in autumn and winter. Male and female plants must be grown together to ensure fruiting 3 × 4ft.

LEFT: *Most sorbus are grown for their red or orange berries, but some also have white or yellow berries, and there is the bonus of spectacular leaf color just before they fall. This is Sorbus 'Joseph Rock'.*

Pyracantha 'Orange Glow'
Evergreen shrub, usually grown against a wall but also an attractive free-standing plant. White flowers in early summer, orange-red berries in autumn and winter. There are other suitable species and varieties 8 × 8ft.

Rhus typhina (syn. *R. hirta*)
Deciduous small tree or large shrub. Large, divided leaves, coloring orange-red and yellow before they fall 10 × 12ft.

Skimmia japonica
Evergreen shrub. Fragrant creamy-white flowers in spring, red berries in late summer and early autumn. Male plant needed to pollinate female 3 × 3ft.

Sorbus
Many species and hybrids make small or medium-sized trees with red or yellow berries and good autumn foliage color. Good ones are *S. aucuparia* and hybrids, *S.* 'Embley', and *S.* 'Joseph Rock'.

ABOVE: Pernettya mucronata *is available with pink and red berries as well as white ones. This variety is* 'Mulberry Wine'.
RIGHT: *Skimmias have long-lasting red berries. This one is* S. japonica 'Nymans'.

VARIETY WITH VARIEGATION

Variegated plants make a border look lighter and more interesting when flowers are scarce, and variegated evergreens are particularly useful at times when little is flowering.

Avoid planting too many variegated plants close together. Use them between other plants with plain foliage where the leaf coloring will be shown off to advantage.

Aralia elata 'Variegata'
Deciduous shrub or small tree. Leaflets margined and marked creamy-white ('Aureovariegata' has a broad, irregular gold margin). White flowers in late summer and early autumn *10 × 7ft.*

Arundinaria viridistriata (syn. *Pleioblastus auricomus, Pleioblastus viridistriatus*)
Bamboo. Dark green leaves broadly striped with yellow. Purplish-green canes *3 × 2ft.*

ABOVE: Hosta fortunei albopicta.
BELOW: *Only a few variegated trees are suitable for a small garden. This is* Aralia elata *'Variegata'.*

Aucuba japonica (variegated varieties)
See *Everbright evergreens.*

Buxus sempervirens 'Aureovariegata'
Evergreen shrub with small leaves which are striped, splashed and mottled pale yellow. 'Elegantissima' has irregular creamy-white margins *4 × 3ft.*

Carex morrowii 'Evergold'
Sedge
Clump-forming with grass-like leaves striped yellow along the center *10 × 12in.*

Cornus alba 'Elegantissima'
Deciduous suckering shrub with red stems and leaves margined and mottled with white. 'Spaethii' is similar but has gold variegation *7 × 6ft.*

Elaeagnus x *ebbingei* 'Limelight'
Evergreen shrub. Large green leaves with a central splash of deep yellow *8 × 7ft.*

Elaeagnus pungens 'Maculata'
See *Everbright evergreens.*

Euonymus fortunei (variegated varieties)
See *Everbright evergreens.*

Fuchsia magellanica 'Versicolor'
Deciduous shrub. Small fuchsia-type flower in summer and into autumn. Gray-green, white, yellow, and pink variegation. Hardy except in cold areas *4 × 3ft.*

Hebe x *franciscana* 'Variegata'
Evergreen shrub, not suitable for very cold areas. Small rounded leaves edged cream. Mauve-blue flowers in summer *2 × 2ft.*

ABOVE: Pachysandra terminalis *is an excellent ground cover for shade, but the plain green form looks rather boring. 'Variegata' is much more interesting.*

LEFT: Houttuynia cordata *'Chameleon'.*

BELOW: Vinca minor *'Variegata'.*

Hostas (many variegated varieties)
Herbaceous perennial 1–2ft ×
1–2½ft.

Houttuynia cordata 'Chameleon'
Herbaceous perennial. Outstandingly striking, heart-shaped foliage, variegated with shades of yellow, green, bronze and red. Small white flowers in summer
12 × 18in.

Hypericum x *moseranum* 'Tricolor'
Evergreen shrub. Yellow flowers about 2in across from mid summer to mid autumn. Green and white leaves edged pink
2 × 2ft.

Ilex (variegated varieties)
See *Everbright evergreens.*

Iris pallida 'Variegata'
Sword-like leaves, striped creamy-white and green. Blue flowers in early summer *2 × 2ft.*

Iris pseudacorus 'Variegatus'
Sword-like leaves striped green and yellow while young, turning greener with age. Yellow flowers in early summer. Although associated with water, it will grow in an ordinary border though it does best in damp soil *3 × 2ft.*

Ligustrum (variegated varieties)
See *Colour themes.*

Pachysandra terminalis 'Variegata'
Evergreen sub-shrub. Green and white leaves. Inconspicuous white flowers in late spring
12 × 18in.

ABOVE: *Variegation is important in the border. This is* Iris pallida *'Variegata'.*

Phormium hybrids
See *Everbright evergreens.*

Salvia officinalis 'Icterina'
Evergreen shrub. Gray-green leaves splashed with yellow
2 × 2ft.

Vinca minor 'Variegata'
Evergreen prostrate shrub. Green and creamy-white leaves. Pale mauve flowers 8in × 2ft.

Weigela florida 'Variegata'
Deciduous shrub. Leaves edged creamy-white. Pink flowers in early summer *5 × 4ft.*

Yucca gloriosa 'Variegata'
See *Everbright evergreens.*

PLANTING FOR QUICK RESULTS

Annuals are almost instant – many are already in flower when you buy them – border perennials are respectable after a year, but shrubs can seem infuriatingly slow to mature.

Not all shrubs are slow-growers, however, so if you want your border to look well established in three years instead of five or even ten, try those suggested here.

Even those plants that grow quickly will leave gaps in the early years. In a mixed border, fill these gaps with the quicker-growing border perennials; in a shrub border add a few bushy annuals.

Bear in mind that some of the shrubs that grow quickly while young may continue to grow (over-enthusiastically) once they've reached what you consider a modest size. The height and spread estimates of the plants listed below are based on three years (though much depends on soil and climate), but they are only likely to grow a little more than this even by 10 years. Those that grow taller can be pruned back hard to restrict their size. *Buddleia davidii*, for example, will be much better if you cut it back hard each spring.

There are many more quick-growers, however, so don't assume that your scope for an almost instant border is limited solely to those listed below.

Aucuba japonica
See *Everbright evergreens*.

Buddleia davidii
Deciduous shrub. Fragrant, usually lilac-blue flower clusters at ends of arching branches, from mid summer to mid autumn. Other colors include shades of red, purple, and white *8 × 5ft.*

Caryopteris x *clandonensis*
Deciduous shrub. Narrow, gray-green leaves. Clusters of bright blue flowers in late summer and early autumn *3 × 2ft.*

Choisya ternata
See *Color themes*.

LEFT: *Tough, low-growing, quick to mature, and very bright in flower are qualities that make* Genista tinctoria *well worth considering. This variety is 'Royal Gold'.*

BELOW: Hypericum calycinum *grows and spreads rapidly, so don't plant it where these characteristics can become an embarrassment. The flowers are bold and beautiful.*

Cistus x *corbariensis*
Evergreen shrub. Dull green leaves wavy at the edge. Bold white flowers with a yellow mark at the base of each petal, in late spring and early summer *2½ × 2ft.*

Cytisus x *kewensis*
Deciduous shrub. Pale yellow, pea-like flowers, in profusion during late spring. Spreading shape *18in × 3ft.*

Philadelphus coronarius 'Aureus'
See *Color themes.*

ABOVE: Leycesteria formosa *is quick-growing, and highly popular with birds. They love the dark purple berries.*
RIGHT: *Weigelas come in a range of colors, but mainly pinks and reds. They grow quickly and flower young.*

Erica carnea
See *Everbright evergreens.*

Fuchsia magallanica
See *Variety with variegation.*

Genista tinctoria
Deciduous shrub. Deep yellow pea-type flowers throughout the summer *2½ × 2ft,* but height tends to be very variable.

Hebe 'Midsummer Beauty'
Evergreen shrub. Pale green leaves, slightly reddish beneath. Sprays of lavender-purple flowers from mid summer to mid autumn. Note this plant is not reliably hardy in cold areas *3 × 3ft.*

Hypericum calycinum
Evergreen shrub. Large yellow, cup-shaped flowers all summer. Can be invasive *18in × 2ft.*

Lavandula (various)
Evergreen shrub. The popular lavender. Gray-green leaves and flowers in shades of blue or purple *2 × 2ft.*

Leycesteria formosa
Deciduous shrub. Cane-like stems forming a bamboo-like clump. Drooping flower tassels containing white flowers with claret bracts, followed by purple-black fruits *5 × 3ft.*

Lupinus arboreus
Short-lived deciduous shrub. Foliage and flower spikes resemble the herbaceous lupin, but the lightly fragrant flowers are much sparser. Usually yellow, but can be lilac to purple or blue. Good for a hot, dry site *4 × 3ft.*

Mahonia 'Charity'
See *Everbright evergreens.*

Potentilla fruticosa
See *Color themes.*

Senecio 'Sunshine'
See *Color themes.*

Spiraea x bumalda
Twiggy deciduous shrub. Flat flower heads, usually crimson, in late summer. Some varieties have variegated foliage *2½ft × 18in.*

Weigela hybrids
Deciduous shrub. Funnel-shaped flowers in late spring and early summer. Mainly shades of red and pink *6 × 5ft.*

BELOW: Spiraea × bumalda (syn. S. japonica). *This is 'Anthony Waterer'.*

NO FUSS, LOW-MAINTENANCE PLANTS

There are plenty of people who do not have a lot of time to tend to their gardens. If you want to save the cost and time involved in regularly replanting with seasonal plants, grow hardy perennials and shrubs. But if you really want to cut down on maintenance, grow only those that are undemanding, with no need to prune regularly, or to keep lifting, dividing, or cutting back.

Most shrubs will require very occasional pruning, perhaps to cut out a dead or diseased shoot, or to improve the shape if growth is not symmetrical, and sooner or later border perennials will benefit from being lifted and divided, but the plants suggested here can be left for many years without attention. They will almost thrive on neglect, yet will not get out of control.

Aucuba japonica
See *Everbright evergreens*.

Berberis thunbergii
There are many varieties, including variegated, purple-leaved and gold-leaved. Shape and height also vary with variety: *B.t. atropurpurea* 'Bagatelle', for example, makes a dwarf rounded ball of growth covered with coppery-red leaves, usually less than *18in* tall and broad, 'Helmond Pillar' is dark purple but grows into a narrow column *4ft* or so high but only about *12in* wide.

Bergenia hybrids
See *Everbright evergreens*.

ABOVE: Cotoneaster horizontalis *can be grown as ground cover or as a climber.*

ABOVE: Cotinus coggygria *is sometimes called the smoke bush because of its flower heads. It can make quite a large shrub in time, but requires minimal attention.*

Choisya ternata
Both green and golden forms (see *Colour themes*) are trouble-free plants if protected from cold winds in winter.

Cornus stolonifera 'Flaviramea'
Deciduous shrub. Green leaves turn yellow before falling. Yellowish-green winter stems *6 × 6ft*.

Cotinus coggygria
Deciduous shrub. Rounded shape with pale green leaves (there are also purple-leaved varieties) that have brilliant autumn colors. Feathery sprays of purple or pink flowers in mid summer *8 × 8ft*.

Cotoneaster
There are many cotoneasters, from ground-huggers to shrubs *10ft* or more tall. *C. horizontalis* (see *Autumn leaves and berries*) and *C. dammeri* (see *Everbright evergreens*), are popular ground-huggers, but many others are suitable for a small garden.

Elaeagnus pungens 'Maculata'
See *Everbright evergreens*.

Erica carnea
See *Everbright evergreens*.

Fatsia japonica
Evergreen shrub. Large, hand-shaped glossy green leaves (there is a variegated variety). White, ball-shaped flower heads that appear on mature plants in mid autumn
8 × 8ft.

Griselinia littoralis
Evergreen shrub. Pale green leaves (there are variegated varieties). Not suitable for cold areas. Slow-growing
10 × 10ft.

Hebes
See *Everbright evergreens.*

Hemerocallis hybrids
See *Color themes.*

Hibiscus syriacus
See *Color themes,* but there are other varieties in different shades of blue, pink, and white.

Ilex
See *Everbright evergreens.*

Kniphofia hybrids
Herbaceous perennial. Large, stiff, poker-like orange or yellow flower spikes. Flowering season extends from early summer right through to mid autumn, according to variety
2–4 × 2–4ft.

Liriope muscari
Evergreen perennial. Clumps of broad, grassy leaves, and spikes of mauve-lilac flowers evident from late summer to mid autumn
18 × 12in.

Mahonia japonica
Evergreen shrub. Glossy, dark green leaves divided into leaflets. Fragrant, lemon-yellow flowers from early winter through to early spring
8 × 8ft.

Pernettya
See *Autumn leaves and berries.*

Potentilla fruticosa
See *Color themes.*

Ribes sanguineum
Deciduous shrub. Drooping clusters of small pink or red flowers in spring
6 × 6ft.

Ulex europaeus
Evergreen shrub. Spiny growth, covered with deep yellow single or double flowers in spring. Flowers may also appear intermittently in winter *5 × 5ft.*

Viburnum davidii
Evergreen shrub. White flowers in early summer. Turquoise-blue berries later if both male and female plants are planted *3 × 4ft.*

Viburnum tinus
See *Everbright evergreens.*

Yucca
See *Everbright evergreens,* but the non-variegated form is equally suitable for a border or as a specimen plant.

ABOVE: *The kniphofias, sometimes called red-hot-pokers, are bold herbaceous border plants. Once well established they make large clumps. Some species are quite small, however, and different varieties flower at different times. Many kniphofias are unhappy in very cold areas and need protection during the winter.*

DON'T FORGET THE DWARF CONIFERS

Conifers need negligible care, and if you choose dwarf species and varieties they will remain compact enough for a small garden. Be cautious about using them in a mixed border, however, as they seldom blend in as satisfactorily as ordinary shrubs.

PLANTS FOR A PURPOSE

ONE OF THE SECRETS OF SUCCESSFUL GARDENING is the ability to choose the right plant for a particular position or use. Plants will always thrive more readily if they are suited to the conditions. Forcing an inappropriate plant into shade if it demands full sunlight, or planting a shade-lover in a scorching suntrap, is a recipe for disappointment.

You will find plenty of ideas for plants that relish problem areas like shade or sun in the pages that follow, but sometimes the question is less which plant suits particular conditions than which fulfils a particular purpose. In the following pages you will find plants that provide the right solution, whether you want a scented shrub, climber for a pergola, or an arresting

ABOVE: *Don't be afraid to grow shrubs and plants such as lilies in pots and tubs as well as the more ubiquitous seasonal summer flowers.*
LEFT: *Climbing and rambling roses are useful for summer screens, but bear in mind that it is only seasonal cover.*

LEFT: *Clematis can be planted in shade provided they can rise above it to flower in the sun.*

OPPOSITE ABOVE: *Ivies will grow almost anywhere, in sun or shade, along the ground or up a wall or tree. Green varieties can be a trifle boring, but variegated varieties are always bright.*

BELOW: *'Exotics' can be used as focal points to bring interest to an otherwise boring area during the summer, but will probably need winter protection.*

'architectural' plant as a focal point.

There are 'exotics', some of which are quite tough, other plants will only thrive during the summer months and you will either have to protect them in winter or treat them as expendable. There are also suggestions of plants to attract wildlife.

If a particular variety has been mentioned, other varieties, perhaps in different colors or with minor variations in size or shape, will almost certainly do well in the same situation. White and pale colors tend to show up better in shade, however, and where possible varieties particularly suited to the conditions have been mentioned.

Be prepared to experiment with plants, especially with those that seem to thrive in similar situations in your area, and concentrate on those that clearly do well. Do not be afraid to abandon plants that fail to live up to expectations.

PLANTS THAT PREFER SHADE

Shade is perhaps the universal problem in small gardens. It is difficult to find a significantly large growing area that is not within the shade of a building or a boundary fence, wall or hedge, for at least part of the day . . . and sometimes there are areas in shade for most or all of the day. Such positions are also often very dry, for obstructions that cast shade also cast a rain shadow.

With the exception of some really difficult areas, there are nearly always some plants that will establish themselves and thrive. In these difficult spots you must be prepared to give the plants a little extra help for the first year. The soil should be enriched with organic material, such as garden compost or rotted manure and fertilizer, but above all the ground must be kept moist. Regular watering in dry spells will be almost essential for the first season. After that, all the plants mentioned here will be able to look after themselves under normal conditions.

Those plants with an asterisk are suitable for dry shade. The others are unsuitable for dry sites, and some prefer moist ground.

Ajuga reptans
Almost evergreen perennial. There are several good varieties with variegated and colored leaves. Short spikes of blue flowers in early and mid summer *6 × 9in.*

ABOVE: Astrantia major *is not an eye-catching plant from afar, but does well in shade.*

ABOVE: Ajuga reptans *is one of those accommodating plants that will thrive in sun or shade, and it will even grow in crevices between paving. There are many varieties that are attractively variegated.*

Astilbe hybrids
Herbaceous perennial. Fern-like divided foliage. Feathery plumes of pink, white, or red flowers *2–3ft × 18in.*

Astrantia major
Herbaceous perennial. Star-like papery-looking white or greenish-pink flowers in early and mid summer *2ft × 18in.*

★*Aucuba japonica*
See *Everbright evergreens.*

★*Bergenia* hybrids
See *Everbright evergreens.*

★*Brunnera macrophylla*
Herbaceous perennial. Rough, heart-shaped leaves. Sprays of blue flowers like forget-me-nots, in late spring and early summer *18 × 18in.*

★*Buxus sempervirens*
See *Variety with variegation.*

Camellia
See *Everbright evergreens.*

Dicentra spectabilis
Herbaceous perennial. Ferny foliage. Pink, red or white heart-shaped flowers on arching stems in late spring and early summer *18 × 18in.*

★*Epimedium perralderianum*
Evergreen perennial. Young leaves bright green marked bronze-red, changing to copper-bronze in winter. Small yellow flowers in early summer *12 × 12in.*

Sarcococca hookeriana humilis
Evergreen shrub. Slender, lance-shaped leaves. Very fragrant small white flowers in winter
2 × 2ft.

Saxifraga x *umbrosa*
Evergreen perennial. Rosettes of green leaves from which sprays of pink flowers appear in late spring and early summer *12 × 12in.*

Skimmia japonica
See *Autumn leaves and berries*.

Symphoricarpos albus
Deciduous shrub. Small, urn-shaped pink flowers from mid summer to early autumn. White berries like marbles from mid autumn to mid winter *6 × 6ft.*

Tiarella cordifolia
Evergreen perennial. Maple-shaped leaves, turning bronze in winter. Feathery spikes of white fluffy flowers in late spring and early summer *9 × 12in.*

Viburnum davidii
See *No fuss, low-maintenance plants*.

Vinca minor
See *Variety with variegation*.

LEFT: Symphoricarpos albus *is a vigorous, spreading shrub, which is best not planted among choice plants, but very satisfactory for a difficult shady position.*

Helleborus
See *Color for the cold months*.

Hosta
See *Variety with variegation*.

Hypericum calycinum
See *Planting for quick results*.

★*Liriope muscari*
See *No fuss, low-maintenance plants*.

Lonicera nitida
See *Color themes*. The all-green species can be used, but the yellow 'Baggesen's Gold' looks brighter in a sunless position.

★*Mahonia aquifolium*
Evergreen shrub. Large, leathery divided leaves. Fragrant yellow flowers in early and mid spring *4 × 4ft.*

★*Pachysandra terminalis*
See *Variety with variegation*.

★*Ruscus aculeatus*
Evergreen sub-shrub. Strong erect stems covered with tough green 'leaves' (actually modified stalk). Inconspicuous flowers in early and mid spring, bright red berries in autumn if male and female plants are present *3 × 3ft.*

ABOVE LEFT: *Here the blue flowers of* Brunnera macrophylla *show up well against a golden conifer.*

RIGHT: Sarcococca hookeriana, *a winter-flowering plant that has unspectacular flowers but an arresting fragrance.*

SUN LOVERS

Sunny spots where the ground is moist, or where the sun is intense for just part of the day before it moves around, present no problem for the majority of plants. All except the shade-loving plants are likely to thrive. But if the position is sunny nearly all day, and the soil tends to be free-draining and dry, you need plants adapted to such bright and arid conditions.

Fortunately, those plants that do well in these positions are often bright, floriferous, and very colorful. As a general rule, gray-leaved plants are well suited to these conditions, but if in doubt check.

Most of the plants suggested here tolerate dry soil well. However, give perennials and shrubs extra attention for the first season. Once they get their roots down they should be able to survive happily in a normal year.

Achillea filipendulina
See *Color themes.*

Agapanthus hybrids
See *Color themes.*

Artemisia arborescens
Semi-evergreen shrub. Silvery-white, much divided leaves. Yellow flowers in early and mid summer. Unfortunately not reliably hardy in cold areas *4 × 4ft.*

Aurinia saxatile
See *Color themes.*

Buddleia davidii
See *Planting for quick results.*

Caryopteris x *clandonensis*
See *Planting for quick results.*

Colutea arborescens
Deciduous shrub. Divided, pale green leaves, and yellow pea-like flowers in summer. These are followed by inflated seed pods, flushed coppery-red *8 × 8ft.*

Convolvulus cneorum
Evergreen shrub. Silvery foliage. Funnel-shaped white flowers, flushed pink beneath the petals, all summer *2 × 2ft.*

Cytisus scoparius hybrids
Deciduous shrub. Green branches make it look evergreen. Pea-type flowers, in shades of yellow, red and pink, many multicolored, in late spring and early summer *8 × 6ft.*

Echinops ritro
Herbaceous perennial. Divided, prickly gray-green foliage, spherical steel blue flower heads in mid and late summer *3 × 2ft.*

ABOVE: *Osteospermums thrive in a hot, sunny situation. This one is* O. jacundum.

ABOVE LEFT: Colutea arborescens *has the bonus of interesting inflated seed pods as well as pretty yellow flowers.*

ABOVE RIGHT: Helianthemum nummularium *hybrids thrive in hot, sunny situations. They come in a variety of color, mainly reds, pinks and yellows.*

OPPOSITE BELOW: Phlomis fruticosa *can be a rather coarse-looking plant, but it thrives in hot, dry soils.*

Eryngium variifolium
Evergreen perennial. Dark green leaves marbled white. Gray-blue flower heads with white collars, in mid and late summer *2ft × 18in.*

Genista tinctoria
See *Planting for quick results.*

Hebe
See *Everbright evergreens.*

Helianthemum nummularium hybrids
Evergreen sub-shrub. Green or gray leaves. Masses of small flowers in shades of red, orange, yellow, pink, and white, in late spring and early summer, with a second flush later in the year if the dead flowers are trimmed off *6–9in × 2ft.*

Kniphofia hybrids
See *No fuss, low-maintenance plants.*

Lavandula
See *Planting for quick results.*

Nepeta x faassenii
See *Color themes.*

Osteospermum hybrids
Evergreen sub-shrub. Still sometimes called *Dimorphotheca.* Large daisy-shaped flowers mainly in shades of purple, pink, and white, all summer. Not hardy in cold areas, but will tolerate frosts where the winters are not severe *1 × 2ft.*

LEFT: Sedum spectabile *has fleshy, succulent leaves, enabling it to grow well even in a hot, sunny position.*

Perovskia atriplicifolia
See *Color themes.*

Phlomis fruticosa
Semi-evergreen shrub. Gray-green foliage. Clusters of quaint, bright yellow flowers at the tips of shoots, in early and mid summer *2½ × 4ft.*

Phormium
See *Everbright evergreens.*

Romneya coulteri
Sub-shrubby perennial. Large fragrant white flowers, *4–6in* across from mid summer to mid autumn. Not recommended for cold areas *4 × 4ft.*

Rosmarinus officinalis
See *Everbright evergreens.*

Santolina chamaecyparissus
See *Color themes.*

Sedum spectabile
Herbaceous perennial. Succulent leaves. Large, flat pink flower heads in early and mid autumn *18 × 18in.*

Stachys lanata
See *Color themes.*

Ulex europaeus
See *No fuss, low-maintenance plants.*

Yucca
See *Everbright evergreens.*

ANNUALS THAT LOVE THE SUN

Most hardy annuals thrive in hot, bright conditions, and especially those with daisy-like flowers that only open when it's warm and sunny. Be generous with the annuals, especially those native to sunny climates such as South Africa.

PLANTS FOR THE TROPICAL LOOK

If you are trying to create a garden based on Mediterranean influences, with white-painted walls and with the emphasis on hot climate flora, you will need to use plenty of plants that give the impression that they are exotic or tender when in fact they are quite frost-tolerant.

Some of the plants suggested here are only hardy enough for warm areas where frosts are light and seldom prolonged, others are really tough.

You can of course use many of them in an ordinary border, but the ones suggested here are primarily effective as part of an area reserved for the more striking plants.

If you live in a cold area and have a greenhouse, conservatory, or even a porch, grow the more vulnerable plants in large pots and move them to this protected area for winter.

Arundinaria viridistriata
See *Variety with variegation*.

Clianthus puniceus
Evergreen climbing shrub. Divided, feathery leaves, crimson-scarlet claw-shaped flowers in early summer. Will only survive outdoors in mild districts. Can reach about *10ft*.

Cordyline australis
Palm-like plant with strap-like leaves at top of plant. *C. a. purpurea* has brownish-purple leaves. Where winters are mild and frost not severe it can be left in the ground and may grow into a tall tree. Elsewhere grow in a pot, where it will remain much smaller. Protect for the winter.

Fatsia japonica
See *No fuss, low-maintenance plants*.

Gunnera manicata
Huge leaves, like a giant rhubarb. In the ground it is large even for a big garden, but you can grow it in a tub or patio pot to restrict its size. Keep very moist, and protect during the winter.

Kniphofia hybrids
See *No fuss, low-maintenance plants*.

ABOVE: Cordyline australis *'Alberti'*.

Lilium hybrids
You can buy bulbs and pot up your own lilies, or buy them when they are about to bloom. These may have been dwarfed chemically and will probably make better container plants. Heights vary.

Osteospermum hybrids
See *Sun lovers*.

Phormium hybrids
See *Everbright evergreens*.

Rheum palmatum
An ornamental rhubarb that reaches *8ft* tall in flower, but the leaves are less than half this height. White or red flowers in early summer.

ABOVE: *For the cost of a packet of seeds you can have a show like this* Ipomoea tricolor *'Heavenly Blue'*.

ABOVE: *Where winters are mild* Zantedeschia aethiopica *can be overwintered outside.*
TOP: *The big, bold leaves of* Rheum palmatum *look very exotic.*

LEFT: *Lilies are quite easy to grow in pots provided you choose suitable varieties.*

Yucca
See *Everbright evergreens*, but the green form can be just as effective as a variegated variety.

Zantedeschia aethiopica
Well-known white calla flowers, popular with florists. Can be kept outdoors where winters are mild, but is usually best grown in a pot and given winter protection. The growth dies down in winter.

Exotic annuals
Some annuals that are regarded as indoor plants can be grown in the garden for the summer.

Among the flowering plants, celosias are always eye-catching, whether you grow the plume-shaped varieties or those shaped like a cock's comb. A mixture will usually include shades of yellow, red, and pink. The coleus is one of the best foliage pot-plants to try outdoors *en masse* – plants are very easy to raise cheaply from seed. The multi colored foliage matches the exotic croton in boldness and color combinations. Make sure they are carefully acclimatized, and don't put them out too early.

Many half-hardy bedding plants are easily raised from seed – try large daisy-like flowers such as arctotis, with flowers in shades of red, orange and pink. Salpiglossis are always eye-catching, and with their velvety, funnel-shaped flowers in shades of red, purple, and yellow, usually prominently veined and marked, certainly have that 'exotic' look.

Portulacas and cleomes (with spidery-looking flower heads) are among the other half-hardy annuals to include. But be sure to make space for *Ipomoea tricolor*, with its big blue flowers often 4in or so across, which are bound to make a real feature climbing up a trellis.

Disposable houseplants
Use flowering pot-plants to add short-term color to your patio. Plants such as gerberas and dwarfed chrysanthemums are inexpensive and generally treated as disposable plants if used indoors. Sink the pot into the soil so that the plant is easily removed after flowering.

ARCHITECTURAL PLANTS

Architectural plants may seem a contradiction in terms, for one implies the rigidity of buildings and structures, the other the informality and fluidity of plant life. The term is often a puzzle to non-gardeners, yet a plant enthusiast will know instantly when an 'architectural' plant is seen.

'Sculptural' plants

'Sculptural' is perhaps a better way to describe those plants, which, though clearly possessing all the natural beauty of any first-rate plant, also have structure and stature, and above all a shape – and perhaps texture – that an architect might be pleased to use to enhance buildings and structures in the same way as a piece of sculpture might be used.

Some herbaceous plants, such as the acanthus, have assumed architectural status – in this case because the acanthus leaf occurs so often as a pattern in classical architecture, but also because the plant has the bold stance and distinctive profile that makes it stand out from the ordinary. Most architectural plants are trees and shrubs, however, with height as well as a distinctive outline. Use architectural plants sparingly and with careful consideration, not as part of a mixed planting but rather as you would large ornaments, as punctuation points within the garden.

Use architectural plants to make a bold statement in paved and gravel gardens, or to break up an otherwise boring area of lawn.

Acanthus spinosus

Statuesque plant with large, deeply divided leaves that are both erect and arching. Mauve and white, hooded flowers on stiff spikes in mid and late summer *3 × 3ft.*

Angelica archangelica

Biennial or short-lived perennial. Large, deeply divided, aromatic leaves on stiff, upright plant. Ball-like head of smaller clusters of yellowish-green flowers in mid and late summer *8 × 3ft.*

LEFT: Acanthus spinosus *is one of those plants with dramatic leaves and equally imposing flowers, and not one that will be ignored.*

BELOW: Angelica archangelica *makes a bold plant about 6ft tall, with large leaves and striking globular flower heads. Use it as a focal-point plant in the herb garden.*

Catalpa bignonioides 'Aurea'

Deciduous tree. The green species is far too large for a small garden, but 'Aurea' is more compact, and can be bought trained as a shrub-like multi-stemmed tree. The golden leaves are very large and handsome *15 × 15ft.*

Cordyline australis

See *Plants for the tropical look.*

Cornus controversa 'Variegata'

A small tree with wide-spreading branches spaced out to give it a layered effect. Leaves have striking silver margins *15 × 15ft.*

RIGHT: *'Charity' is one of the most imposing hybrid mahonias, with bold sprays of yellow flowers through the coldest months of the year.*

LEFT: *Daturas (now more correctly called brugmansias) are ideal for the summer patio as they have to be taken indoors for winter frost protection.*

Crambe cordifolia

Herbaceous perennial. Normally a plant for a large garden, but sparsely planted it will make a bold statement. Enormous leaves and huge clouds of gypsophila-like small white flowers in early and mid-summer *6 × 6ft.*

*Datura (*syn. *Brugmansia)*

Tender shrub. Must be overwintered in frost-proof place, but often grown on patio in a large tub for summer. Large drooping leaves, big bell-shaped very fragrant flowers – usually white or cream, but there are also red and pink kinds *6 × 4ft* when grown in a tub.

Fatsia japonica

See *No fuss, low maintenance plants.*

Gunnera manicata

See *Plants for the tropical look.*

Juniperus scopulorum 'Skyrocket'

Conifer. You may also find it sold under the name of *J. virginiana* 'Sky-rocket'. Very narrow, pencil-like growth. Typical conifer foliage *15 × 2½ft.*

Kniphofia

See *No fuss, low-maintenance plants.*

Mahonia 'Charity'

See *Everbright evergreens.*

RIGHT: Salix matsudana *'Tortuosa' is a small tree that can be as fascinating in winter as in summer.*

Paulownia tomentosa

A large tree totally unsuitable for a small garden. It can be grown as a large shrub, however, by annual hard pruning close to ground level, when the leaves become huge. Treated like this height will be about *8–10ft* and spread about *6ft.*

Phormium hybrids

See *Everbright evergreens.*

Salix matsudana 'Tortuosa'

A small to medium-sized tree with spiralling and twisted stems as well as contorted leaves. Seen at its best in winter when the stems are bare *15 × 15ft.*

Yucca

See *Everbright evergreens*, but a green form is just as useful as a variegated variety as an architectural plant.

LIVING SCREENS

The screening plants described here are not rows of tall conifers or large windbreaks along the boundary, which are inappropriate in a small garden, but plants that you can use to screen objects within the garden and plants that you would be happy to grow as ornamentals too.

Generally, something that requires screening will need it the year round, so evergreens naturally predominate in any list of screening plants. But sometimes a summer-only screen is acceptable. For a summer screen within the vegetable plot, consider Jerusalem artichokes, which provide excellent summer cover and a crop to harvest at the end of the season!

When looking for a good screening shrub, check that it is well clothed at the base. If you are prepared to erect a trellis or internal fence, many of the plants described under *Climbers and wall shrubs* will also make excellent internal screens. A trellis covered with sweet-smelling honeysuckle will make a summer screen that is pleasing to the eye and the nose. The most popular – and best – honeysuckles are deciduous, so don't expect winter cover, but some fragrant climbing honeysuckles, such as *Lonicera japonica*, are evergreen or semi-evergreen so you will have winter cover as well as summer scent – though at the price of less spectacular flowers.

Trellises and screen block walls

Sometimes it is possible to screen an unsightly object, such as a storage tank with just two or three well-chosen shrubs. Alternatively, erect a trellis or screen wall, carefully integrated as part of the garden design, then use climbers, wall shrubs or ordinary shrubs against these. This double-masking is often the most effective because you have a whole range of climbers that can be used on a trellis, including the ubiquitous but very practical and evergreen ivy, and wall shrubs such as pyracanthas.

Garage walls

Detached garages can dominate a small garden, so you probably need to soften the impact of the walls. Climbers are a natural choice, as are wall shrubs. But you could use a garage as an ideal backdrop for espalier or fan trained fruit trees.

Many evergreen shrubs will do an excellent masking job in front of a garage wall. Let hedging plants such

ABOVE: Griselinia littoralis *'Dixon's Cream'*.
LEFT: Griselinia littoralis.

as *Lonicera nitida* 'Baggesen's Gold' or a golden privet (such as *Ligustrum ovalifolium* 'Aureum') grow up untrimmed until the required height has been reached. Don't attempt to clip these like a formal hedge, but prune over-enthusiastic growth occasionally, and leave them with a natural shape.

Arundo donax
Grass. Forms tall, almost bamboo-like clump, with drooping blue-green leaves. There is also a variegated form 8 × 4ft.

Buxus
Be careful not to choose a dwarf form if you want a taller screen. This is a classic shrub to clip to shape, and is much used for topiary as well as hedges. You could clip your screen to shape.

Griselinia littoralis
See *No fuss, low-maintenance plants.*

Ilex
See *Everbright evergreens.*

Ligustrum ovalifolium 'Aureum'
See *Color themes.*

Lonicera nitida 'Baggesen's Gold'
See *Color themes.*

Miscanthus sacchariflorus
A large grass. Narrow, arching leaves, forming a dense clump 8 × 3ft.

Polygonum baldschuanicum
Now more correctly *Fallopia baldschuanica.* Deciduous climbing shrub. A vigorous climber, but instead of using it as a screen up a trellis, try letting it grow over the eyesore itself, if it is an old shed, for example. Within a few years it will almost cover it. Profusion of small white or pale pink flowers in conspicuous sprays from mid summer to early autumn. Height and spread is usually dictated by its support.

PERMANENT PLANTS FOR CONTAINERS

The choices and permutations for summer bedding plants to use in containers are almost endless. Every year there are new varieties of seed-raised plants, and growers re-introduce some of the old and neglected tender perennials to keep up the supply of novelties.

On this page you will find ideas for permanent plants to try – those that will form part of the framework of the garden, summer and winter. Use them alongside, and not instead of, seasonal flowers. You might even be able to plant spring bulbs and summer annuals around the base of some of the shrubs suggested.

Agapanthus
See *Color themes.*

Camellia
See *Everbright evergreens.*

Ceratostigma willmottianum
See *Autumn leaves and berries.*

Choisya ternata 'Sundance'
See *Color themes.*

Clematis, large-flowered
Deciduous climbing shrub. Large flowers in a wide range of colors. Avoid the rampant species in a container. Try growing them in a half-tub, as described opposite.

Cotoneaster 'Hybridus Pendulus'
Deciduous shrub, grafted to form a small weeping tree. Small white flowers in early summer. Red berries in autumn *6 × 3ft.*

Laburnum
Small deciduous tree. Produces long tassels of yellow pea-like flowers in late spring and early summer *8 × 6ft.*

Laurus nobilis
Evergreen shrub. The popular kitchen herb, sweet bay. Sometimes attractively trained and clipped into a formal shape. About *6ft.*

Mahonia 'Charity'
See *Everbright evergreens.*

ABOVE: Choisya ternata *'Sundance',* *an excellent garden plant and attractive in a large container.*
TOP: *Agapanthus are excellent tub plants, but need winter protection in cold areas. This variety is* 'Delft'.

RIGHT: Camellia . *'Adolphe Audusson'.*

Miscanthus sinensis 'Zebrinus'
Grass. Forms a dense clump of vertical stems that unfurl at the top into narrow, reflexed leaves, with distinctive yellow bands. Grows to an approximate height of *4ft* when contained in a large tub or a half-barrel.

Rhododendron
Evergreen shrub (some azaleas are deciduous). There are many rhododendrons and azaleas

(botanically types of rhododendron) dwarf enough to be grown in a container. An ericaceous soil mix is essential for good results. Color and size depend on variety.

Rosmarinus officinalis
See *Everbright evergreens.*

Salix caprea 'Pendula'
Deciduous weeping tree. Also known as *Salix* 'Kilmarnock'. Small, umbrella-shaped tree with stiffly pendulous branches. Attractive catkins in spring.

Taxus baccata
Conifer. The popular yew, but choose a golden form such as 'Aurea'. This makes an irregular cone in outline. If you prefer a slimmer, more pencil-shaped profile, try *T. b.* 'Fastigiata Aurea'.

Viburnum tinus
See *Everbright evergreens.*

Yucca
See *Everbright evergreens.*

LEFT:
Rhododendron *'Loder's White'* in a clay pot decorated with masonry paint.

HOW TO PLANT A CLEMATIS BARREL

A clematis barrel can look really stunning when well established. You can choose several varieties to flower at the same time, or different ones that will flower at different times and so extend the period of interest, but bear in mind that this could make pruning more difficult.

1 Fill a half barrel or other large container with a loam-based soil mix. You need a large, deep container and heavy potting mixture which will support the canes as well as the plants.

2 Plant about three to four clematis in a barrel of this size. Angle the root-ball so that the plants point slightly inwards.

3 Secure the canes at the top. Tie them with string or use a purchased plastic cane holder. Don't worry if the growth reaches the tops of the canes, it will just tumble down again and make the planting look even more dense.

CLIMBERS AND WALL SHRUBS

Small gardens almost inevitably have a lot of potential space for climbers and wall shrubs. Often there are external fences or walls that can be covered, interior surfaces, such as trellises, which can be used as screens, and nearly always there are all the walls of the house. Some will be in sun for most of the day, others will remain mainly in shade, but there are plants to suit every aspect.

Where space is at a premium, the vertical space provides a wonderful opportunity to grow more plants. Climbers and wall shrubs have a small 'footprint', and if pruned or trained so that they do not encroach too far out from the support, it is usually possible to grow other plants in front of them.

The climbers suggested here are all shrubs that will form a permanent part of the garden framework, but supplement them with annual climbers for a little extra variety and color. Most annuals can be grown up a trellis – and they should be happy in a container if there is no soil in which they can be planted.

The heights given in the following list are an indication of how tall they are likely to grow in a small garden. Many climbers grow as high and wide as their support. Some clematis will grow to more than 30ft with a suitable support – such as a tree – but settle for 4ft if that is the height of a fence, and grow along it instead.

Actinidia kolomikta
Climber for wall or pergola. Dark green heart-shaped leaves tipped with white and pink. Sun or partial shade *10ft.*

Ceanothus
Wall shrub. Blue flowers in late spring or early summer, or in late summer and into autumn, depending on species. Some are evergreen, others deciduous. Some are of border-line hardiness where winters are cold. Sun *10ft.*

RIGHT: *Clematis remains one of the most popular climbers. This is 'The President'.*

Clematis
An impressive deciduous climber. Use large-flowered hybrids against a trellis on a wall. Vigorous species such as *C. montana* can be grown along a fence or through a tree. Sun or partial shade. Large-flowered hybrids *10ft.*

Euonymus fortunei
See *Everbright evergreens.*

LEFT: Actinidia kolomikta.

Garrya elliptica
Evergreen wall shrub. Grown for its long catkins in late winter and early spring. Shade or sun *8ft*.

Hedera
The ivies need no introduction. Choose large-leaved kinds, such as *H. colchica* 'Dentata Variegata', for a pergola or arch, small-leaved varieties of *H. helix* for a wall or fence. Shade or sun *10ft*.

Humulus lupulus 'Aureus'
Herbaceous perennial climber. Golden leaves. Pergola or arch. Sun or partial shade *10ft*.

Hydrangea petiolaris
Vigorous climber. Flat heads of white flowers in early summer. Shade or partial shade. Needs tall wall or a tree *20ft*.

Jasminum nudiflorum
See *Color for the cold months*. Shade or partial shade. Best against a wall, perhaps secured to a trellis *10ft*.

Jasminum officinale
Climber. Fragrant white flowers in summer and often into autumn. Pergola or arch *10ft*.

Lonicera x *japonica*
Evergreen climber. White or pale yellow fragrant flowers from early summer to mid autumn. 'Aureoreticulata' has yellow-veined leaves. Best supported against pergola or fence *20ft*.

Lonicera periclymenum
Deciduous climber. Very fragrant flowers, pale yellow flushed purple-red, ideal for pergola, arch, or trellis. Some varieties flower in late spring and early summer, others from mid summer to early autumn *10ft* but can grow much taller up a tree.

Polygonum baldschuanicum
See *Living screens*. Fence or wall.

Pyracantha
Wall shrub. White flowers in early summer, red or orange berries in autumn and into winter. Sun or shade *10ft*.

Rosa
Climbing and rambling roses need no description or introduction. There are many to choose from, and some are excellent for pergolas, arches, and against the wall around the door. Many are very fragrant. Sun or partial shade *10ft*.

Vitis coignetiae
Deciduous climber. Large leaves with beautiful autumn colors. Sun or shade. Will grow very tall in a tree but can be contained on a pergola.

ABOVE: *Pyracantha – a good wall shrub.*
ABOVE LEFT: Jasminum nudiflorum.
TOP: Garrya elliptica.

Wisteria
Deciduous climber, with long drooping tassels of blue or white flowers in late spring and early summer. *W. sinesis* and *W. floribunda* are both widely grown, and are suitable for a pergola, or to grow against a house wall. Sun or partial shade *10ft*, but can be much taller.

PLANTING FOR SCENT

A garden without scent is like a meal without seasoning. All the elements appear to be there, but that extra spice is missing that lifts it from the ordinary and heightens the senses.

You can overdo the seasoning, however, so avoid planting too many fragrant plants of the same kind close together. One scent will compete with another, and the more subtle ones may be lost. Rather, make sure that plants with very fragrant flowers are chosen to flower in succession over a period of months. It will not matter if two fragrant shrubs are planted side by side if one flowers after the other has finished.

Mix plants that flower in the day with those that are scented at night – perhaps a rose that gives off its heady perfume during the day with a honeysuckle or night-flowering nicotiana that comes into its own once dusk falls.

Make use of plants with aromatic leaves that release their fragrance when brushed against or deliberately crushed.

Some of the plants suggested here are ornamental plants in their own right – roses and honeysuckles are highly decorative as well as fragrant – but find space for some plants which flower at night. Although they will add nothing to the daytime display they will certainly make up for lack of visual impact by their wonderful perfume after dark.

Chimonanthus praecox
See *Color for the cold months*.

Choisya ternata
See *Everbright evergreens*. The green variety is just as good for fragrance.

Cytisus battandieri
Large deciduous shrub. Gray leaves. Pineapple-scented yellow flower in late spring and early summer. Unfortunately not reliably hardy in cold areas, and best grown as a wall shrub *10 × 8ft.*

Daphne mezereum
Deciduous shrub. Red, pink, purple or white flowers between late winter and mid spring *4 × 3ft.*

Hamamelis mollis
See *Color for the cold months*.

Jasminum officinale
See *Climbers and wall shrubs*.

Lavandula
See *Planting for quick results*.

Lonicera periclymenum
See *Climbers and wall shrubs*.

Mahonia 'Charity'
See *Everbright evergreens*.

Rosa
Roses are among the most fragrant of all shrubs, and you can grow their many forms in beds, borders, and as climbers. Use roses lavishly for a fragrant garden. Heights vary according to species.

ABOVE: *Stocks – varieties of* Matthiola incana – *are worth planting for their fragrance.*
LEFT: *One of the strongest spring fragrances comes from* Daphne mezereum *'rubra'.*

FRAGRANT ANNUALS

If you use a lot of summer bedding plants, be sure to include some fragrant ones such as stocks (*Matthiola incana*), and ornamental tobacco plants (nicotiana hybrids), though bear in mind that many of the compact, day-opening varieties of nicotiana have nothing like the powerful scent of the taller, evening-scented ones.

Night-scented stocks (*Matthiola bicornis*) are totally unattractive by day, so grow these as a gap-filler in a border where their day-time appearance doesn't matter.

Philadelphus
Deciduous shrubs. Several good species and hybrids, have fragrant white flowers in early summer.

Sarcoccoca hookeriana humilis
See *Plants that prefer shade.*

ABOVE: *Lilacs (varieties of* Syringa vulgaris*) are among the most fragrant shrubs, and although some grow tall they are not too large for a small garden.*

Skimmia japonica
See *Autumn leaves and berries.*

Spartium junceum
Deciduous shrub. Yellow, pea-type flowers throughout the summer 8 × 6ft.

Syringa vulgaris
Deciduous shrub, the popular lilac. The varieties have very fragrant flowers mainly in shades of blue, purple, mauve, and white, in late spring and early summer 8 × 5ft.

Viburnum x *bodnantense*
See *Color for the cold months.*

Wisteria
See *Climbers and wall shrubs.*

SCENTED FOLIAGE

Use some of the scented-leaved geraniums (pelargoniums) on the patio. You can even plant some of them at the front of a border. Many herbs, such as pineapple sage, lemon balm, and lemon verbena, make acceptable patio plants in pots.

Among the shrubs with aromatic foliage are *Artemisia arborescens*, *Choisya ternata*, *Laurus nobilis*, *Rosmarinus officinalis*, and *Salvia officinalis*.

Eucalyptus can be grown in a small garden if you prune it back hard each spring to grow like a shrub.

RIGHT: *Wisterias are grown mainly for visual impact, but they are also fragrant.*

ATTRACTING WILDLIFE

You don't have to turn your garden into something that resembles a meadow – some might say overgrown and weedy garden – to attract wildlife.

Lots of shrubs, border and rock plants, and annuals and biennials will attract wildlife of many kinds, from birds, bees and butterflies to wasps and weevils. Not all are welcome, of course, but for the few that you don't want to attract you will certainly gain many beautiful and beneficial animals that will help to control the pests.

You will, of course, need to create particular habitats if you want to encourage particular types of wildlife, such as a pond for aquatic creatures. And there is a lot to be said for leaving an area of grass long – perhaps where bulbs are naturalized if you want a horticultural justification – and if you let a few nettles grow behind the garden shed you will provide food plants for many kinds of caterpillars that will later grace your garden as butterflies.

Attracting wildlife in general often brings the bonus of more beneficial insects such as hoverflies and ladybirds, which will help to keep down pests such as aphids.

LEFT: Aucuba japonica *'Variegata'*.

ABOVE: Berberis thunbergii *'Atropurpurea Nana'*.

Shrubs
Aucuba (birds)
Berberis (birds, bees, butterflies)
Callicarpa (birds)
Ceanothus (bees)
Cistus (bees)
Cotoneaster (bees, birds)
Cytisus (bees)
Daphne (birds, bees)
Escallonia (bees)
Hebe (butterflies)
Hedera (bees, butterflies)
Hypericum (birds)
Ilex (birds)
Lavandula (bees, butterflies)
Leycesteria formosa (birds)
Ligustrum (bees, butterflies)
Lonicera periclymenum (butterflies)
Mahonia (birds)
Pernettya (birds)
Perovskia (bees)
Potentilla (bees)
Pyracantha (birds, bees)
Rhamnus frangula (bees, butterflies)
Ribes sanguineum (bees)
Skimmia (birds, bees)
Symphoricarpos (birds, bees)
Syringa (bees, butterflies)
Ulex (bees)
Viburnum (birds, bees)
Weigela (bees)

Border and rock plants
Achillea filipendulina (bees, butterflies)
Armeria maritima (bees, butterflies)
Aster novi-beglii (bees, butterflies)
Aurinia saxatilis (butterflies)
Erigeron (bees, butterflies)
Nepeta (bees, butterflies)
Scabiosa caucasica (bees, butterflies)
Sedum spectabile (bees, butterflies)
Solidago (birds, bees, butterflies)
Thymus (bees, butterflies)

Annuals and biennials
Centaurea cyanus (bees, butterflies)
Dipsacus spp (birds)
Helianthus annuus (birds)
Hesperis matronalis (bees)
Limanthes douglasii (bees)
Lunaria annua (birds)
Scabious annual (bees, butterflies)

LEFT: Sedum *'Autumn Joy'*.

BELOW: Solidago.

ABOVE: Aurinia saxatilis.

OTHER WAYS TO ATTRACT WILDLIFE

A thick hedge attracts far more wildlife than a fence or wall. A prickly evergreen hedge like holly will provide good nest and roost sites for many birds.

An old log pile provides refuge for many beneficial insects and can make a nest site for small mammals.

the KITCHEN GARDEN

AMBITIOUS KITCHEN GARDENS ARE SELDOM achievable in a small space. Vegetables that are hungry for space such as potatoes and cabbages may lose out to flowers. But if you are content with smaller vegetables such as lettuces, carrots, beets, and dwarf beans, and can relegate tall climbing beans and expansive plants like globe artichokes to the mixed or herbaceous border, it is quite practical to grow a wide range of vegetables even where space is quite restricted.

Grow a whole range of vegetables, from lettuces to peas, in containers like windowboxes

ABOVE: *Raspberries are not an ideal crop for a small garden but they can be trained so that they don't take up too much space.*

TOP: *Fruit-growing is possible even on a roof or balcony garden . . . with a little imagination.*

OPPOSITE: *This picture shows an interesting way of providing supports for tall vegetables in a small kitchen garden.*

LEFT: *One of the upright-growing apple trees ideal for a small garden or limited space. This variety is 'Walz', planted in a bed of 'Surrey' ground cover roses.*

and growing bags. Even potatoes can be harvested from pots and growing bags and tomatoes of all types have been grown with great success in growing bags. This kind of small-scale vegetable gardening is demanding, and the yields always very modest for the effort involved, but if the idea of harvesting your own fresh vegetables just before you pop them into the pot appeals, you may find it worth the effort. It can certainly be fun.

If you have a reasonably sized garden – large enough to divide off a section for a kitchen garden – growing them in the ground is the most practical way to produce your vegetables, and much of the fruit.

Fruit trees and bushes are often ornamental and can be easily integrated into the flower garden. Trained fruit trees like espalier and fan apples look attractive even with bare branches in winter.

Herbs are much more easily accommodated than vegetables. Many are highly ornamental and lots of them make good container plants. Others look perfectly in place in a border. If you want to make a real feature of your herbs, make a herb garden a key part of your garden design.

ORNAMENTAL HERBS

Formal herb gardens look impressive, but can be difficult to accommodate in a small space. However, as the illustrations below show, there are alternatives.

Bear in mind that though herb gardens are packed with interest in summer, in winter you will be left with just a few evergreen shrubs and a handful of herbs that retain their foliage and are tough enough to survive unprotected. Alternatively, incorporate your herbs in an overall garden design that carries interest through all the seasons. Here are some other ways to incorporate herbs in a small garden.

A collection in a container
A herb pot can hold half a dozen or more different herbs. Do not start to harvest until plants are growing strongly, then keep harvesting little and often to produce compact yet well-clothed plants.

Shrubby plants like bay and rosemary can be grown in tubs to decorate the patio or to display by the front or back door.

Windowbox herbs
Herbs can be grown in windowboxes and troughs provided you choose compact plants such as thymes and marjorams. Ornamental, variegated mints also look good.

Growing bags
Growing bags are not elegant, but they are useful for rampant plants like mints, which would otherwise make a take-over bid for the border.

In among the flowers
Many herbs are so decorative that they don't look amiss in beds and borders, and indeed some are planted more for their ornamental than culinary uses.

Among the herbs that look good with other border plants are chives, fennel, marjoram, and lemon balm.

ABOVE: *Have fun with your small herbs. They can be arranged informally in pots, or grouped together, as in the small wheelbarrow.*

RIGHT: *An attractive herb collection can be grown in a small raised bed, but bear in mind that many of these plants will grow much larger.*

HOW TO MAKE A HERB WHEEL

If you have an old cartwheel, just paint or varnish that and set it into the ground ready to plant. Few of us have access to cartwheels, however, but an acceptable second best can be made from bricks. Adjust the size of the wheel to suit your garden. Bricks are a convenient way to make the 'spokes', but you could use dwarf dividing 'hedges' of hyssop or thyme. Place an attractive terracotta pot in the center as the hub of the wheel, and plant with herbs, or place an upright rosemary in the center. A rosemary may become too large after a few years, but either keep it clipped to shape and size or replace it every second or third year.

1 Mark a circle about 5–6ft across, using a line fixed to a peg to ensure an even shape. If it helps, use a wine bottle filled with dry sand instead of a stick to mark out the perimeter. Excavate the ground to a depth of about 6in.

2 Place the bricks on end, or at an angle, around the edge. If you place them at a 45 degree angle it will create a dog-tooth effect; bricks placed on end will look more formal. Either lay them loose in compacted earth, or bed them on mortar.

3 Lay rows of brick, cross-fashion, as shown. If the diameter does not allow for them to be laid without gaps in the center, stand an ornament or pot in the middle if you are not planting directly into the soil in that position.

4 Fill the areas between the spokes with good garden or potting soil.

5 Plant each section, using plants that will balance each other in size of growth if possible. You could, for instance, grow a collection of different thymes.

6 For an elegant finish, carefully cover the soil with fine gravel.

FRUIT IN A SMALL SPACE

The most satisfactory way to grow tree fruits such as apples and pears in a small garden or a confined space is trained as a cordon, fan or espalier against a wall or fence. Even some bush fruits such as gooseberries can be trained as cordons or double cordons against a fence.

Blackberries and hybrid berries can be trained against a fence or over an arch, but keep the growth contained and avoid allowing thorny shoots to overhang pathways.

It is even possible to grow apples in pots on the patio, but with the new flagpole-type varieties available that grow in a narrow column, you may prefer to plant these where space is limited. They will require much less watering and attention than ordinary varieties on dwarfing rootstocks in pots.

The initial training of espaliers, fans and cordons demands patience and skill. Unless you particularly like the challenge and can wait for two or three years longer, it is best to buy a ready-trained tree.

ABOVE: *Wall-trained fruit trees take up relatively little space.*
RIGHT: *If you want apples in a small garden it is best to use one of the columnar varieties or to grow an ordinary variety on a trained system like this espalier 'Lord Lambourne'.*

BUYING FRUIT TREES

Whether a fruit tree such as an apple, peach or cherry is suitable for a small garden depends not so much on the variety of the fruit but on the rootstock. This has a profound effect on the size of the tree (as well as how soon it starts to fruit). Always check the rootstock before you buy, and if in doubt ask whether it is suitably dwarfing for a small garden.

TRAINED FRUIT TREES

Trained trees look attractive and produce a heavy crop from a restricted space. But they require regular and methodical training, sometimes twice a year. If in doubt about how to prune a particular trained fruit, consult an encyclopedia or fruit book.

Espaliers are more ornamental than cordons (some shrubs, such as pyracanthas, are occasionally trained as espaliers using the same methods).

Cordons are usually trained at an angle of about 45 degrees, secured to support canes and wires fixed to stout posts or to a fence. Many plants can be planted in a small space, and soft fruits such as gooseberries and red and white currants can be trained in this way, saving the space taken up by a bush form.

Fans can be free-standing, tied to wires supported by posts, but they are usually planted against a wall or fence. In time a fan can be trained to cover a large area, such as a garage wall.

Step-overs are single-tiered espaliers, used as a fruiting edging, perhaps within the kitchen garden.

Potted fruit

Apples can be grown in pots provided you choose a very dwarfing rootstock. The same applies to peaches. You can experiment with other bush and tree fruits, but bear in mind that this is second best to growing them in the ground.

Flagpole apples

You can buy a range of apple trees that rarely produce long sideshoots, but instead grow upright and produce most fruiting spurs along the main vertical stem. These take up little space and won't cast a heavy shadow, so they are ideal for growing in a flower bed. The blossom is pretty in spring, and the ripening fruits are ornamental later in the year.

Rhubarb chard

Rhubarb chard is ornamental enough to be grown in the flower border. You can even grow it in a large pot as a foliage plant for the patio, though this may not be the best way.

ABOVE: *This rhubarb chard is growing in a flower bed.*

ABOVE: *There is always space for a few strawberries if you grow them in a container like this.*

Strawberries

If you don't have much space for fruit, you can still try growing strawberries. A strawberry barrel or a tower container will hold a lot of strawberries and provided you keep the container well watered it will be laden with fruit – which won't become splashed with mud if the weather is wet, and will be easy to pick. Also, the fruit will be more difficult for slugs to reach.

FINDING ROOM FOR VEGETABLES

If you are really restricted for space, and the lure of fresh home-grown vegetables is strong, you can grow them in containers. Wherever possible, however, it is better to grow them in the ground.

If you simply don't have space for a vegetable plot, quite a lot of vegetables can be grown in beds and borders intermixed with ornamental plants.

The 'vegetable plot' should never be tucked away in a dull, sunless part of the garden. Most vegetables need good light and plenty of moisture to do well. Dry ground shaded by hedges and walls seldom produces succulent vegetables.

Among the flowers

It is quite possible to incorporate vegetables as part of a formal bedding scheme – red or purple rhubarb chard leaves contrast well with gray foliaged bedding plants, carrot foliage doesn't look unattractive as a foil for bright summer bedding plants, and even a red or green leaved cut-and-come-again (oak leaf) lettuce such as 'Salad Bowl' will make a pretty edging for a bed of summer bedding. Unfortunately the problem comes at harvest time. When gaps soon become rather conspicuous in a formal bedding scheme.

ABOVE: *This raised vegetable bed in a flower garden makes an interesting feature as well as a productive area.*

Vegetables are more acceptable as gap fillers in the herbaceous or mixed border. They fill the space admirably, and after harvesting the border is left no less attractive than it was originally. Suitable candidates are lettuces, radishes, beets, asparagus, peas, carrots, leaf beet, and spinach, but much depends on the size of the space and your imagination.

Ornamental potagers

The term potager comes from *jardin potager*, simply being French for kitchen garden. But the term has come to refer primarily to a kitchen garden – usually with both fruit and vegetables – laid out ornamentally, perhaps with beds edged with low

LEFT: *Ornamental kales are usually grown for their decorative effect, but they are edible if you get tired of looking at them! This variety is 'Coral Queen'.*

hedges like a parterre. Treated like this, your kitchen garden can become a prominent design element in the small garden.

Growing bags

Growing bags are excellent for vegetables if all you have is a balcony or patio on which to grow them. It is quite feasible to grow lettuces, spinach, radishes, cucumbers, tomatoes, turnips, even self-blanching celery and potatoes, in growing bags.

Clearly, you won't keep the family fed with potatoes from a couple of growing bags, and the economics don't make much sense. But it is worth planting an early variety (you can always move the bag into a protected area if frost threatens) so that you can enjoy those first few new potatoes straight from the garden . . . or patio . . . or balcony.

ABOVE: *These are 'Totem' tomatoes growing in a 10in pot.*
BELOW: *You can even grow tomatoes in a hanging basket.*

Dwarf peas, another unlikely-sounding crop, can also be grown successfully in a growing bag.

Troughs, tubs and pots

Tomatoes are one of the most successful crops for a growing bag, and they are equally successful in pots provided you choose a suitable compact variety.

Squashes and cucumbers are also a practical choice for a tub or large pot. Potatoes can be grown in a large pot for a bit of fun, but you might be better planting an eggplant or pepper in it.

Windowboxes and baskets

The only vegetable likely to do well in a hanging basket is the tomato, but you must choose a trailing or drooping variety, and maintain excellent control over both watering and feeding.

Windowboxes offer more scope, and apart from tomatoes (again, a dwarf or trailing variety is essential), stump-rooted carrots, radishes, onions, and lettuces are among the crops that do well.

Rather than grow a hearting lettuce, which leaves a gap as the whole head is harvested at once, try a non-hearting, cut-and-come-again variety that you can harvest in stages.

INDEX

ABOVE: *Pots often look best when grouped.*

ABOVE: *Penstemons.*

ABOVE: *Birdhouses can add interest.*

ABOVE: *Ornaments bring life to dull corners.*

ABOVE: Chimonanthus praecox.

ABOVE: *Tiny corners can be packed with interest.*

BELOW: *Bold features are for small gardens too.*

ABOVE: *This corner of a small garden shows how the clever use of plants, and the addition of a focal point, can bring impact to an unpromising position.*

ACKNOWLEDGEMENTS

The publishers would like to thank the following for their generous help in the production of this book:

Mr & Mrs Blackadder, Judith Blacklock, Nick and Jenny Brunt, Mr and Mrs Richard Chilton, Mrs Eadie, Brand and Sheila Inglis, Mr and Mrs Norman Moore, Joan Parkinson, Vera Quick, Jean Rankin, Peggy Robinson, Audrey Simons, Mrs Shacklock, Chris Sharp, Derek Waring and Dorothy Tutin, Steven Woodhams, Ginny Worsley and Helen Yemm for allowing us to photograph their gardens; Anthony Gardiner of Gardiners Herbs, 35 Victoria Road, Mortlake, London for his help with sourcing locations; Andy and Neil Sturgeon of The Fitted Garden and Acorn Landscaping, Garson Farm Garden Centre, Winterdown Road, Esher, Surrey, KT10 8LS for providing the locations, materials and equipment for the step-by-step photography.

The publishers would also like to thank the following picture libraries for allowing us to reproduce their photographs:

Key: t = top; b = bottom; l = left; c = centre; r = right

Peter McHoy for the pictures on pages 12b, 36t, 37t, 46t, 46b, 48t, 53bl, 57br, 60t, 60b, 61bl, 62b, 63t, 63b, 66b, 67t, 70, 71t, 71b, 79, 86bl, 88t, 88b, 95b, 97b, 98t, 98bl, 98br, 99t, 114t, 114c, 114b, 115t, 115c, 115b, 116t, 116b, 117t, 117c, 117b, 118t, 118b, 119t, 119c, 119b, 120t, 120b, 121t, 121bl, 121br, 122t, 122b, 123tl, 123tr, 123bl, 123br, 124t, 124b, 125tl, 125tr, 125b, 126t, 126b, 127, 130tc, 130b, 131t, 131m, 131b, 132tr, 132tl, 132b, 133t, 133b, 134t, 134b, 135tr, 135br, 135l, 136t, 136b, 137tl, 137tr, 137b, 138l, 138r, 139t, 139b, 140t, 140c, 140b, 141, 142t, 142b, 143t, 143bl, 143br, 144t, 144b, 145t, 145b, 146, 147t, 147c, 147b, 148bl, 152r, 153l, 153r, 154b, 155t, 157b and 158b. The Harpur Garden Library for the pictures on pages 2 (*Count and Countess Labia, Cape Town*), 4 (*designed by Simon Fraser and Sara Robinson*), 6 (*designed by Maggie Geiger, NYC*), 11t (*A garden in Canterbury*), 11b (*designed by Michael Balston*), 13b (*designed by Arabella Lennox-Boyd*), 15t (*Nooroo Mt. Wilson, NSW*), 17b (*designed by Trevor Frankland*), 17t (*designed by John Patrick, Vic*), 24b (*designed by Anthony Noel, London*), 28t (*designed by Berry's Garden Co., Golders Green*), 29b (*designed by Christopher Masson*), 30t (*designed by Malcolm Hillier, London*), 40 (*designed by Christopher Masson, London*), 42b (*designed by Wayne Winterrowd & Joe Eck, London*), 43b (*designed by Anne Alexander-Sinclair*), 44t (*designed by Ernie Taylor, Great Barr*), 44b (*A garden in Tayside*), 48t (*designed by Berry's Garden Co., Golder's Green*), 52t, 52b (*designed by Hilary McMahon for Costin's Nursery, RHS Chelsea*), 59b (*designed by Anthony Noel, London*), 59t (*Fudlers Hall, Mashbury*), 62t (*designed by Jan Martinez, Kent*), 67b (*designed by Bruce Kelly, NYC*), 75br (*designed by Arabella Lennox-Boyd*), 82b (*designed by Anne Alexander-Sinclair*), 84br (*designed by Lalitte Scott, NYC*), 86br (*designed by Phillip Watson, Fredericksburg, Va*), 90b (*designed by Simon Fraser, London*), 96t (*Joe Elliot, Broadwell, Gloucs*), 100 (*designed by Beth Chatto*), 101 (*designed by Ernie Taylor, Great Barr*), 104 (*Bank House, Borwick*) and 109t (*Home Farm, Balscote, Oxon*). The Garden Picture Library for the pictures on pages 12t (*Marijke Heuff*), 38 (*Ron Sutherland*), 54 (*John Duane*), 78 (*Jane Legate*), 150t (*Lynne Brotchie*) and 150b (*J S Sira*). Jacqui Hurst for the pictures on pages 14, 73t, 90t, 91t, 91bl, 103t, 103b, 105t, 112tl, 128l and 129t. Derek Fell for the pictures on pages 5, 15b, 31t, 39t, 39b, 69tr, 101, 149 and 154t. Robert Harding for the picture on pages 28b and Lucy Mason for the picture on page 95.